Also by Ernestine D. Motouom

Modern Slavery: The Story of My American Dream

IDOL WORSHIP IN CHRISTIANITY

Idol Worship in Christianity:

The Corruption of Faith by Pagan Practices

Ernestine D. Motouom

© 2020 by Ernestine D. Motouom

All rights reserved. This book or any portion thereof may not be reproduced or used in any manner whatsoever without the express written permission of the publisher except for the use of brief quotations in a book review.

ISBN: [978-0-578-71438-7]

Ernestine D. Motouom may be contacted by email: kmkouokam@gmail.com.

To my brother Sidoine, my sister Odile,
and my in-law Billy, with love

Table of Contents

Prologue · xi
Introduction · xv
Chapter 1 True Worship versus Idol Worship · · · · · · · · · · · · · · 1
Chapter 2 The First Ungodly Family · 11
Chapter 3 The Devil's Fall · 25
Chapter 4 My Personal Experience—from Idol Worshipper to
 Born-Again Christian · 45
Chapter 5 Should Christians Celebrate the End-of-Year Festivals? 67
Chapter 6 Other Religious Festivities Borrowed from
 Babylonians · 83
Chapter 7 Passages Found in the Bible That Condemn Carved
 Objects Called gods · 93
Conclusion · 179
Acknowledgments · 181
References · 183

Prologue

THE PURPOSE OF THIS BOOK is to summarize what the Bible says about idols and worship briefly.

This book's narrative came from my personal experiences as a once-fervent Catholic votary and then a born-again Christian. It furnishes fascinating verses from the Bible as well as with Reverend Alexander Hislop's early twenty-first-century discoveries, published in a book entitled *The Two Babylons*.

Idol worship is at the heart of most religious groups around the world and several Christian denominations. Regardless of religion, they all have the same root and a similar mode of worship. The grandson of Noah—Nimrod and his mother Semiramis, are at the center of all religions except for the faith of the real children of God delivered by Jesus Christ.

In the beginning, the true, living God created the world and all it contains. He created Adam and Eve on the sixth day and assigned to them the duties of cultivating the garden and worshiping him. Everything went well until the fall of humankind, causing sin to enter the world. Then Cain, upon killing his brother Abel, departed from God's presence and began the first ungodly family. Apart from God, all human desires are evil. The wickedness of humanity became overwhelming, which led God to destroy all the living creatures living on the earth at that time through the flood, sparing only Noah—the only godly man of his time—his family, and the few chosen pairs of animals.

After the flood, his grandson Nimrod became great among his people. He was the first king ever on earth. Besides, he was the first man to organize people into communities and to build cities. He engineered and built the Tower of Babel. He was also the first to subdue a horse. He was a mighty hunter before the Lord.

Not only did Nimrod amaze the people over whom he ruled, but he also, unfortunately, drove them into a slimy pit. Mad at God for destroying the world, which in that early age had brought the Lord's fear into the souls of Noah's sons and grandsons, Nimrod wanted to free his people from such fear. Therefore, in an act setting him apart as the greatest apostate ever, he set forth the doctrine of freedom to do whatever one pleased without fear of God or judgment. He initiated the worship of Baal, which is transcribed in *the Babylonian Mystery Religion*. Consequently, his uncle murdered him, cut apart his body, and sent a part thereof to every city to warn those who followed in Nimrod's path.

Unfortunately, his adepts continued the mystery in secret, because he had set them free from the fear of judgment. They also began to worship Nimrod himself as a god and then, his mother/wife, who received the title "queen of Heaven." After the destruction of the Tower of Babel, the worship of Nimrod spread all over the world; even in this present time, he is still worshipped in virtually all religious denominations around the world under different names.

Shockingly enough, some Christian denominations have adopted and grafted worship methods from pagans whose god is Nimrod. Christmas, Easter, and Halloween, for example, are of pagan origin. Nimrod was born on the twenty-fifth of December. *Easter* is of Chaldean origin and means *Astarte*—both of which were monikers of the goddess Venus in Syria and Cyprus. More importantly, every single dogma in the Catholic Church, and many of its festivals, borrow their roots from the pagan worship of Nimrod and his mother, including the Lady Day, the Feast of Saint John, confession of sins to priests, penance, and so forth.

The coming of Jesus to earth intended to restore humankind to God; to convert them to true worship and adoration (as opposed to the human-made belief system initiated by Nimrod and his mother); and to redirect their path away from the human tradition of the worship of idols that cannot speak, hear, or see. Since the beginning of the world, the real, living God spoke to Adam and Eve in the Garden of Eden, he talked to Moses, and even in the New Testament and till the present day, he speaks to his devoted worshippers. In Acts 10:3–6, God spoke to Cornelius and sent him to Peter, while in Acts 10:19–20, he prepared Peter in a dream to receive Cornelius, who was then baptized along with his family. Cornelius was a devoted Roman centurion, yet he believed in God. This speaking God stands in contrast with the mute, deaf idols people call "gods."

Paul warns, "See to it that no one takes you captive through hollow and deceptive philosophy, which depends on human tradition and the elemental spiritual forces of this world rather than on Christ" (Col. 2:8).

Introduction

AT THE BEGINNING OF THE world, God created humans, singled them out among other creatures, and bestowed upon them a special love. He made them in his image and gave them unique knowledge and understanding. With that, he drew humanity to himself from the beginning. The first couple was placed in the garden to cultivate it and to worship their Creator. Although some may say that the call to worship does not transpire in the garden, God spells out a call to obedience and worship when he commands Adam, "You are free to eat from any tree in the garden; but you must not eat from the tree of the knowledge of good and evil, for when you eat from it, you will certainly die." (Gen. 2:16–17).

They did an excellent job for a time keeping that command, until the devil, in the form of a snake, deceived Eve, marking humanity's fall. Sin entered the world, and everything was turned upside down. The course of society was changed and altered. Nothing was ever the same. Adam and Eve were chased from the garden, the perfect world. Their everyday duties went from cultivating the garden and harvesting holy fruits planted by the Holy One, the Almighty himself, to the hard work of plowing the soil, fighting with weeds and thorns, and waiting for the harvest. The only duty left unchanged was the call to worship their God. The Bible recalls that the first couple and their children worshipped God. While they lost the privilege and luxury of life in the garden and their closeness to God, they did not lose their entire relationship with him.

It is important to notice that worship in the garden and worship outside it were performed differently. I am not sure exactly how worship was performed in the garden, or whether there was a special time and place of adoration and worship. The Bible does not provide precise details on the topic; but it does highlight that once the first couple were out of the garden, the act of worship—unlike worship in the garden—was expressed through offerings of what their own hands had worked for:

> "Now Abel kept flocks, and Cain worked the soil. In the course of time Cain brought some of the fruits of the soil as an offering to the Lord. And Abel also brought an offering—fat portions from some of the firstborn of his flock. The Lord looked with favor on Abel and his of-fering, but on Cain and his offering he did not look with favor. So, Cain was very angry, and his face was downcast." (Gen. 4:2-5)

We know that they worshipped God, for he revealed himself to them through the exchanges of words from time to time. Since God communicated with them and gave them instructions, they did not have any reason to doubt the existence of the supreme, almighty Being that had created them, the world, and the universe.

So how did doubt of his existence takes place and linger in the minds of humans to the point where some denied his existence, fashioned their gods by human hands, or adopted polytheistic beliefs? How did holy worship in the garden and immediately following the first couple's banishment transition into the idol worship that has defiled religious adoration and worship through the centuries to this day? I have a hard time understanding how someone can carve an object with their own hands and crown it "god." What *is* God?

Over the course of this book, we are going to explore the Bible and try to find answers.

CHAPTER 1
True Worship versus Idol Worship

WHAT IS TRUE WORSHIP? TRUE worship is done in spirit. However, many belief systems have come short in comprehending the meaning of true worship; instead, they use objects as the primary tool in their worship practices. Most belief systems are non-Christian religions, but they also include a few Christian denominations. I will focus my attention solely on Christian churches, mainly the Roman Catholic Church, of which I was once a devoted member.

I know from experience that members of some denominations, including Catholicism, long dearly to read the Bible. However, something—a strange force that is difficult to explain and comprehend, or some sort of discouragement or lack of energy—kicks in and either puts them to sleep or distracts them, and before they realize it, they move on to something else without investing much time in the Bible. This talk is not a mere presumption or paranoia of mine; as a former Catholic believer, I have experienced it, and some of my close friends and relatives still in that church have testified to this. After I left the Catholic Church, through the confession of idolatry I had committed, my chain fell off. I was set free, and I could freely read the Bible. Since 2002, the year I was born again, I have already read the Bible from page one to the end four times. Even this is extremely poor engagement, especially compared to the devotion of those who read the whole Bible every year. Thumbs up to them.

Being idle whenever the Bible is opened is a hurdle that has kept Catholic votaries from discovering the real mystery hidden in it; instead, their knowledge remains limited mainly to what is preached from the pulpit on Sundays. I am here to remind them that Rome's institution chooses a limited and narrow selection of passages to be read in its churches and does not embrace every topic discussed in the Bible. Among the issues overlooked is idolatry, which priests will never mention in the pulpit in any form or fashion, though it is one of the most foolish things humanity does and irritates God beyond imagination. For ages, the Catholic denomination has endorsed the philosophy that clergy are the only class of people who have the wisdom and knowledge to understand and to interpret the Bible.

According to Reverend Alexander Hislop in his work *The Two Babylons* (2010, 7), they have borrowed this belief from the primitive Babylonian religion established by Semiramis, who was worshipped as Rhea, the great mother of the gods. Babylonians represented her with an image of a woman holding a cup in her hand, and the Bible speaks about her as well.

> "The woman was dressed in purple and scarlet, and was glittering with gold, precious stones

and pearls. She held a golden cup in her hand, filled with abominable things and the filth of her adulteries. The name written on her forehead was a mystery: Babylon the great, the mother of prostitutes and of the abominations of the earth." (Rev. 17:4)

She established a hall of prostitution, and participants were to drink a cup of a mysterious beverage made of wine, honey, water, and flour, which aimed to intoxicate them, put them into a dormant state, and stimulate their passion (Hislop, 7). In some form of initiation conducted by the priests, participants made a secret confession of their sins. This confession was mandatory, and without it, the process of initiation would be interrupted (9). The Babylonian priests were granted authority and power over the understanding and interpretation of writs, myths, and symbols, and participants were told that without a complete and total capitulation to the priests, salvation could not be granted (7). Does this not sound like the papacy, which claims that there is no salvation outside the Catholic denomination?

I wonder how the training of Catholic priests has been carried out until the present time. I wonder whether, during their training, the books they use are also selected in a manner to keep them as blind as they appear to be—to conceal from them those passages that warn against the worship of idols. I wonder if a priest has ever taken the time to read the Bible from Genesis to Revelation. These are the savviest and intellectual people under the sun. How can they fail to grasp the true nature of worship? The Apostle Paul stresses this in his letter to the Romans.

> "Although they claimed to be wise, they became fools and exchanged the glory of the immortal God for images made to look like a mortal hu-man being and birds and animals and reptiles. Therefore, God gave them over in the sinful desires of their hearts to sexual impurity for the degrading of their bodies with one another. They exchanged the truth about God for a lie and worshiped and served created things rath-er than the Creator—who is forever praised. Amen. Because of this, God gave them over to shameful lusts. Even their women exchanged natural sexual relations for unnatural ones. In the same way the men also abandoned natural relations with women and were inflamed with lust for one another. Men committed shameful acts with other men and received in themselves the due penalty for their error ." (Rom. 1:22–25)

We know for sure that some men of God in the Protestant churches have fallen into the sin of having relations with other men; however, this sin is more prevalent among priests in Catholic Churches and has become the mode of life in that inner circle. In October 2020, Pope Francis openly endorsed gay relations despite the apostle Paul's warnings to Romans against that type of lifestyle.

I am on a mission here to shed light on my brothers' and sisters' path still in the Catholic Church. Given their inability to concentrate and read the Bible for themselves, I have taken the time to go through the Holy Bible and select for them every single passage that condemns carved objects. Whatever name you give to your object—Baal, Moloch, Buddha, Mary, or Jesus—true worship was never intended to be that way.

In the Bible, Jesus's disciples once asked him about the signs of his second coming and the end time. In reply, he warned them, "Watch out that no one deceives you. For many will come in my name, claiming, 'I am the Messiah,' and will deceive many" (Matt. 24:4). We know from scripture that toward the end of time, the beast or anti-Christ will claim to be the Messiah, will put his image in the third temple that will be rebuilt, and force people to prostrate themselves before his hand-made image in worship—as the Catholic Church has been doing through the ages. The very presence of the beast's carve image in the holy temple is called "the abomination that causes desolation" (24:15).

Satan introduced idols in worship to anger and irritate the only true living God and lead people astray from true worship. In so doing, Satan is preparing people to readily embrace and accept the call of worshipping his own carved image when the time comes. This abomination will be a smooth move for many religions on earth, which have, for ages, been accustomed to the practice of idol worship. They will not see any problem in it; it will be an easy move from one shape and type of idol to another.

The Bible foretells that those who will refuse to worship the image of the beast will be captured, tortured, and killed. That is why Jesus calls for those who will be living in Judea at the time to run for their lives.

> "So, when you see standing in the holy place "the abomination that causes desolation," spoken of through the prophet Daniel—let the reader un-derstand—then let those who are in Judea flee to the mountains. Let no one on the housetop go down to take anything out of the house. Let no one in the field go back to get their cloak. How dreadful it will be in those days for pregnant women and nursing mothers! Pray that your flight will not take place in winter or on the Sabbath. For then there will be great distress, unequaled from the beginning of the world until now—and never to be equaled again." (Matt. 24:15–21)

The hand-made gods that have taken root in humankind's worship were sought by Satan to defy the Almighty and to drive humanity away from their Creator. After Satan first sinned, God had punished him to eternal damnation in the lake of fire; but after his fall, he vowed not to perish alone. He is at work till this day, deceiving people with all sorts of tricks and deceptions, trying to drag as many people as possible with him to hell.

This is my call: be smart and worship your Creator in spirit and in spirit only; in the name of Jesus Christ, amen! As a taste of what I am talking about, read Isaiah's accounts of true and false worship:

The Lord, Not Idols

> "This is what the Lord says—
>   Israel's King and Redeemer, the Lord Almighty:
> I am the first and I am the last;
>   apart from me there is no God.
> Who then is like me? Let him proclaim it.
>   Let him declare and lay out before me
> what has happened since I established my ancient people,
>   and what is yet to come—
> yes, let them foretell what will come.
>   Do not tremble, do not be afraid.
> Did I not proclaim this and foretell it long ago?
>   You are my witnesses. Is there any God besides me?
> No, there is no other Rock; I know not one.
>
> All who make idols are nothing,
>   and the things they treasure are worthless.
> Those who would speak up for them are blind;
>   they are ignorant, to their own shame.
> Who shapes a god and casts an idol,
>   which can profit nothing?

People who do that will be put to shame;
>   such craftsmen are only human beings.
Let them all come together and take their stand;
>   they will be brought down to terror and shame.

The blacksmith takes a tool
>   and works with it in the coals;
he shapes an idol with hammers,
>   he forges it with the might of his arm.
He gets hungry and loses his strength;
>   he drinks no water and grows faint.
The carpenter measures with a line
>   and makes an outline with a marker;
he roughs it out with chisels
>   and marks it with compasses.
He shapes it in human form,
>   human form in all its glory,
>   that it may dwell in a shrine.
He cut down cedars,
>   or perhaps took a cypress or oak.
He let it grow among the trees of the forest,
>   or planted a pine, and the rain made it grow.
It is used as fuel for burning;
>   some of it he takes and warms himself,
>   he kindles a fire and bakes bread.
But he also fashions a god and worships it;
>   he makes an idol and bows down to it.

Half of the wood he burns in the fire;
> over it he prepares his meal,
> he roasts his meat and eats his fill.

He also warms himself and says,
> "Ah! I am warm; I see the fire."

From the rest he makes a god, his idol;
> he bows down to it and worships.

He prays to it and says,
> "Save me! You are my god!"

They know nothing, they understand nothing;
> their eyes are plastered over so they cannot see,
> and their minds closed so they cannot understand.

No one stops to think,
> no one has the knowledge or understanding to say,

"Half of it I used for fuel;
> I even baked bread over its coals,
> I roasted meat and I ate.

Shall I make a detestable thing from what is left?
> Shall I bow down to a block of wood?"

Such a person feeds on ashes; a deluded heart misleads him;
> he cannot save himself, or say,
> "Is not this thing in my right hand a lie?"
> (Isa. 44:6–20)

Given the length of the Bible and the fact that these passages are scattered throughout, my goal is to collect them in a few pages to be easy to reach and more enjoyable to read. Chapter 7 will be dedicated to the rest of such passages.

CHAPTER 2

The First Ungodly Family

WE SEE FROM SCRIPTURE THAT after Cain killed his brother Abel, he was chased away from God's presence. As a result, he had no relationship with God whatsoever. Cain, like many of us today, was someone who despised discipline. After he had disappointed God with his poor offering, and before he had killed Abel, God had warned him to watch out and to run from sin.

> "Then the Lord said to Cain, "Why are you an-gry? Why is your face downcast? If you do what is right, will you not be accepted? But if you do not do what is right, sin is crouching at your door; it desires to have you, but you must rule over it." (Gen. 4:6–7)

Had Cain listened to God's warning, he wouldn't have fallen into the devil's trap; but he did not listen and instead committed the first murder. Consequently, he was cut off from his Creator. This is what sin does to humans: it separates us from God, and the more we sin, the further we go from him.

At Creation, God had set humans apart and had given them unique knowledge and understanding. Why cannot humans apply this knowledge to understand and distinguish sin from righteousness and apply their hearts to do good? There are two logical explanations: either sin overpowered human beings at the fall, crushing them and inclining their hearts to sin from birth, and/or Satan is at work, deceiving humans so that he might defile and destroy God's work.

The same warning Cain received and did not heed is found in the New Testament and applies to us today: "Be alert and of sober mind. Your enemy, the devil, prowls around like a roaring lion looking for someone to devour" (1 Pet. 5:8). The devil's work is primarily to drive people away from their Creator, and he has been successful.

Genesis 4:26 mentions that after Adam's third son, Seth, gave birth to his first son, people began to call on the name of the Lord. This implies that between this time and Adam and Eve's departure from the garden, there was a time of no worship; after all, Cain—the only son Adam and Eve had left until Seth's birth—had departed from God and was living an ungodly life with his family.

Still, the rebirth of worship did not gain momentum. Instead, more people were driven away from God by their own desires and by the devil's schemes. About seven hundred years later, the only righteous man on earth was Enoch, to whom the Almighty granted an amazing departure from this earth—without transitioning through death or an unpleasant decay. The ultimate punishment of sin after the fall was death, but "Enoch walked faithfully with God," so as a reward, God spared him; instead of dying, he was simply "no more, because God took him away" (Gen. 5:24).

The rest of humanity continued to fall further from God. About nine hundred years later, "the Lord saw how great the wickedness of humans had become on earth and that every inclination of the thoughts of the human heart was only evil all the time," so "the Lord regretted that he had made human beings on the earth, and his heart was deeply troubled" (Gen. 6:5–6). As a result, he flooded the earth, saving only Noah and his family, for he found Noah to be "a righteous man, blameless among the people of his time, and he walked faithfully with God" (6:9).

When we walk away from God, He erases our names from the book of life and remembers us no more. In Genesis 4, Cain and his descendants' genealogy are briefly mentioned, but the next chapter lists the other sons of Adam in greater detail, providing the exact age when they gave birth to their first sons and the actual age when they died. Furthermore, many years had passed between the fall to the flood; many generations had come and gone; many people had been born and had died, but they have all been lost in the crowd. There are no mentions of their names. However, God has pointed his finger to Enoch and Noah, the godly people of their time, lifting them as standards and as examples to follow, highlighting the rewards given to those who follow him: absolute protection in times of trouble and eternal life with him.

I want to underline the grace and goodness of God. He lifted Noah up as a holy man of his time. However, he did not save him alone; he saved Noah's wife and all their children and their wives as well. The Bible never states that Noah's family members were godly people, yet they were saved. Therefore, hanging out with good and faithful people is recommended. Watch with whom you walk. Some blessings may come your way just from choosing the right company. As people say, bad companions corrupt good manners.

After the flood, God blessed Noah and his family and commanded them to multiply and to fill the earth. Among the grandsons of Noah was Cush, whose son Nimrod was said to be a mighty warrior on earth and mighty hunter before the Lord (Gen. 10:8–9). The Bible highlights Nimrod's position as a king who built great cities. How about his genealogy? The Bible is silent about that. As is the custom in the Bible, faithless people are mentioned only briefly. In the lines below, Nimrod is presented as the great apostate, the one who put into place the god Baal. After his death, his disciples continued to worship Baal and gave Baal all Nimrod's attributes when he was alive. His worship has been scattered all over the world to the present time under different names—Moloch, Osiris, Tammuz, Ninus, Saturn, Khons, Orion, and Krishna. His wife, Semiramis, was also deified as a goddess.

The aim of the Bible was to point toward the coming Messiah, so that he could stand out of the confusion and wrong religious practices that had been orchestrated by the descendant of Noah. Since the fall in the garden of Eden, God had placed a curse on the serpent, Satan, saying, "I will put enmity between you and the woman and between your offspring and hers; he will crush your head, and you will strike his heel" (Gen. 3:15). This foretold the Messiah's death, when he would save humankind by means of the serpent's attack, for deliverance could only come through the death of the deliverer.

As it has been the culture for human beings to leave behind their legacies, Adam and Eve surely passed down to their children the promise of Eden. I can imagine his children sitting around him and listening to those stories over and over. The promise of Eden was transmitted down from one generation to the next, appearing in every mythology and culture around the world, and it is exhibited by the sculpture of the Greek god Apollo, shown slaying the head of a serpent, or by the picture of Hercules stepping on the head of a snake (Hislop, 60).

In those early days, people lived in fear of God's judgment, given the fresh memory of the flood (Hislop, 52). This feeling was quite evident, normal, and understandable. For some, tragedy is a catalyst for positive change; for others, it brings about negative, impulsive responses. Nimrod's response to the flood was the latter. On the one hand, in the middle of this confusion and chaos, Nimrod stood up as king and accomplished mighty things. For example, he was known as the first to subdue horses and was identified as the one who subdued or tamed leopards and who wore leopard's skin to show his might. His followers looked at him with awe (44, 47). Moreover, he hunted down wild beasts (which was a treat to the people of his time), organized his people to live together in communities, and built walls to surround the cities so that people felt safe and protected from wild animals. This warranted him great popularity, respect, and renown (51).

On the other hand, Nimrod took it upon himself to free his people from the fear of the Lord. He cast away the fear of judgment that had gripped them after the flood, which granted him the titles of "deliverer" and "emancipator" (Hislop, 51–52). In his great zeal and arrogance, Nimrod defined life in terms of freedom, pleasure, fun, joy, and happiness and led men astray from God, letting them believe it was ok to live without God and still enjoy life. This was the first instance of the philosophy of humanism, and many rallied behind the new approach (53).

This resonates well with the world's creed today, which encourages people not to abstain from anything that makes them feel happy and good. Keeping the law of God means practicing discipline and restraint from all sorts of sins, which conflicts with carnal desires, but Nimrod wanted to be freed from such restraining laws and willfully indulge himself in all pleasurable things flesh desired. Under his shadow, his adepts carelessly distanced themselves from God; they acted as if God did not care or even see when they broke his laws. This denial stimulated a sense of liberty and freedom to do whatever pleased them and to find good and joy solely in sensual pleasures, with no fear of judgment (Hislop, 53–55).

Throughout the years, people have always been inclined to follow bad habits. The path to perdition looks smooth and sweet because the devil wants it to entice more people to take pleasure in things they shouldn't. That is why the Bible says the way to perdition is broad.

Glory be to God in the highest who does not want to lose any of his children. Throughout all time, he has spared some to himself. Not everyone joined Nimrod's club. Nimrod's uncle Shem is believed to have stood against him and plotted his murder. He then had his body dismembered and sent parts of his body into every city where his doctrine was established to warn those who walked in his path (Hislop, 66). However, Nimrod's adepts did not quit; instead, they turned the whole system into what was probably the world's very first secret society (56).

In societies like this, members are bound to keep their deeds forever secret. However, the Bible declares that "there is nothing concealed that will not be disclosed or hidden that will not be made known. What you have said in the dark will be heard in the daylight, and what you have whispered in the ear in the inner rooms will be proclaimed from the roofs" (Luke 12:2–3). Let no one be fooled. On judgment day, everything will be revealed in the broad light of day.

Due to the popularity, honor, respect, and esteem, Nimrod had gained during his life, his wife, Semiramis (who might also have been his mother, for some images portray her as a woman carrying her son in her hands), wanted him to be worshipped as a god and granted him the title of the "woman's promised seed" (Hislop, 58)—the very Messiah promised by God in the Garden of Eden. This promise was well known, and Semiramis used the opportunity of Nimrod's death to present him as the promised son "who was destined to bruise the serpent's head, and who in doing so, was to have his heel bruised" (59). With this misrepresentation began the worship of Nimrod on earth till the present day. He masquerades in most religions worldwide as the Messiah and in the Catholic Church as Jesus. Given the exploits of Nimrod on earth, it was an easy scheme to portray him as having given his life freely for the good of humanity (62), usurping the role of Jesus, who was still to come. Nimrod was elevated to godhood, and Semiramis earned the title of "goddess Mother"; carved images of both were worshipped with great zeal (69).

Nimrod apparently was a black man, but his complexion became a stumbling block for some with time. In order to get past that obstacle, some of his followers put forth a fable purporting that he had been reincarnated into the fairly-complected entity Tammuz (Hislop, 69).

As time went by, Semiramis was also elevated to a place of divinity and was granted the same honor as that of her son in symbols of worship, including images found in the Tower of Babel as well as Greek images of the goddess Diana. In Babylon, a woman's sculpture is shown holding a serpent's head; in Greece, she holds a headless snake (75–76). Hislop attests that the people of the time believed (as the Roman Catholic Church also believes) that the "woman herself" would "bruise the head of the serpent" (75).

As history evolved, Semiramis worshippers began to boldly declare that she had miraculously conceived her son, and they gave her the new title of "virgin mother" (Hislop, 75). This narrative about a virgin mother who gave birth to a great deliverer thus emerged before the true virgin mother, Mary, birthed Jesus Christ, the only real Savior (76). Hislop stressed that "the primeval promise that the 'seed of the woman should bruise the serpent's head' naturally suggested the idea of a miraculous birth" (77), so it is not surprising that the devil influenced humankind to take all the attributes of his fierce enemy, Jesus, and to bestow them upon a mere human being. The devil knows the scripture well.

In Genesis 11, the people of Nimrod's time gathered and built the Tower of Babel, for they longed to reach heaven. Consequently, God came down, confused their languages, and scattered them all over the world. Given that Nimrod was the sole king on earth, he was undoubtedly the one who oversaw and conducted that tower's construction. By the time it was destroyed, his apostasy had taken deep root among his followers; when they had scattered, they had carried with them the practice of idolatry and the way of living they had learned. In his research, Hislop found proof to link Nimrod to the gods worshipped in many countries around the world to this day. For example, the main characteristic of Nimrod as a "huntsman" or the "god of the chase" is attributed to the god Khons of Egypt and Concus, the Latin god of horsemanship (41). In Egypt, as highlighted by Hislop, the priests in their duties were called to wear robes made of leopard skin; Hislop adds that in keeping with the general principles of idolatry, a high priest serving a specific god would indeed wear its insignia (45). Hislop adds that some coins made in Babylon depicted the "centaur, half-man, half-horse, that figures so much in the Greece mythology," and he explains that this "imaginary creation…was intended to commemorate the man who first taught the art of horsemanship" (41–42).

As far as rituals are concerned, the Egyptian god Osiris is worshipped in the same manner as the Greek god Bacchus (Hislop 2010, 48), and all these gods worshipped in various countries have a common representation: a child worshipped in the arms of the goddess-mother, who holds both a cup and a branch. According to Hislop, the cup "exhibited him as the god of drunken revelry, and…orgies" (48); the branch exhibited him as the metaphorical branch of Cush, Nimrod's father (50).

Nimrod was slaughtered by his uncle Shem, and in countries where Nimrod is worshipped, myths reflect this in their depictions of lamentation for a god who was killed. For example, Venus bitterly lamented the death of Adonis, the famous huntsman; "the women of Egypt wept for Osiris; the Phoenician and Assyrian women wept for Tammuz;" and "in Greece and Rome, the women wept for Bacchus" (Hislop, 56). Ezekiel even writes that at "the entrance of the north gate of the house of the Lord," he "saw women sitting there, mourning the god Tammuz" (Ezek. 8:14). These practices were detestable in the sight of God. As the people of Israel distanced themselves from the almighty God, he exposed their deeds and swore to deal with them severely.

Furthermore, the light that encircles the head of the idol of Jesus as depicted by Catholic Church was likewise found on the images of the Babylonian god and goddess, and this symbol of the sun is also found on the head of Apollo (who is believed to be the child of the sun), as well as on the head of the idol of the Roman Madonna (Hislop, 87).

In every culture, the entire royal family is customarily granted favor and great esteem. Semiramis was indeed looked upon as unique and was much respected while her son/husband was still alive, and after Nimrod died, she seized the opportunity to elevate herself even higher as she declared that Nimrod had been the "woman's promised seed"—in other words, the messiah—which earned her the title of "Mother god." Was she purposely manipulating people to gain her divine title? Regardless of her intention, she became a symbol of worship around the world.

Her worship is even seen in Buddhist culture, whose tradition (also before Christianity) speaks of a virgin who would give birth to a son, who would be a blessing to the world. The worship of mother and son in Tibet and China also shares attributes with the Roman Madonna or *Deipara Viergo* (the glorification of the virgin), who was also given the name of "virgin mother of god" (Hislop, 77). Wikipedia (2019) explains that the "Madonna is the representation of Mary, either alone or with her son Jesus." In Egypt before Christianity, this inscription was found on Hathor's temple, the goddess: "I am all that has been, or that is, or that shall be, no mortal has removed my veil. The fruit I have brought forth is the Sun" (77), as her son also was worshipped as the sun god Ra. Mark stressed in his article entitled "Hathor" (2009) that the god "Hathor" was later associated with Isis.. In Greece and Rome, she was given the name, "the dwelling place," and "Tabernacle" in India and Babylon (78). She was found to be worshipped in Germany as well as in Great Britain (81). After the birth of Christianity, instead of putting the goddess-mother aside, her name was simply changed to Virgin Mary, and her worship was then masqueraded and sealed among professing Christians, using the same methods and practices of worship (82). Given all the evidence highlighted by Hislop, he concluded that "the Madonna of Rome is just the Madonna of Babylon" (83).

In the '90s, I learned from Gervais Mendo Ze—a renowned Catholic from Cameroon—that a new Bible was soon to be published, in which Mary would be granted divinity. I am not sure if such a Bible has come out yet, but even if it has, most Christians in that church do not read the Bible anyway. How will they know? Will members bluntly agree and adhere to that doctrine because of the insanely purported infallibility of the pope? Or is it, as Hislop proclaimed, already transcribed in the Roman Catholic dogma? Do lay members simply remain unaware or overpowered and put to sleep by a spirit that makes them gullible and denies them the ability to think, reason, and understand? Does this spirit harden them against change so that they desire only to live and die Catholic? (I will elaborate more on this in my testimony in chapter 4.)

How can someone kneel before a carved object and murmur prayers yet deny that this is idolatry? They are lying to themselves. I remember a song we used to sing. It goes like this, translated from French:

> By your side, good Mother,
> Your children are kneeling.
> Hear our prayers and look down on us with
> favor.

I have only bad memories of singing songs like this. I cannot believe I never recognized the perfume of blasphemy in this song or in the song entitled "Souverain Pontiff." Gervais Mendo Ze wrote this in honor of John Paul II when the pope visited Cameroon in 1995, and we sang it repeatedly. The word *sovereign* is a characteristic only of our Lord, the Creator of the universe; attributing this quality to a mortal—thereby elevating him to a place of honor like that of God—is nothing short of blasphemy.

CHAPTER 3

The Devil's Fall

LET'S TAKE A LOOK AT Ezekiel 28:13–19 from the Bible from NIV:

> "You were in Eden,
>   the garden of God;
> every precious stone adorned you:
>   carnelian, chrysolite and emerald,
>   topaz, onyx and jasper,
>   lapis lazuli, turquoise and beryl.
> Your settings and mountings were made of gold;
>   on the day you were created they were prepared.
> You were anointed as a guardian cherub,
>   for so I ordained you.
> You were on the holy mount of God;
>   you walked among the fiery stones.
> You were blameless in your ways
>   from the day you were created
>   till wickedness was found in you.

> Through your widespread trade
>   you were filled with violence,
>   and you sinned.
> So, I drove you in disgrace from the mount of God,
>   and I expelled you, guardian cherub,
>   from among the fiery stones.
> Your heart became proud
>   on account of your beauty,
> and you corrupted your wisdom
>   because of your splendor. So, I
>   threw you to the earth".

In this speech given by God and dictated by Ezekiel, we see that Satan was beautifully made and adorned with all sorts of precious stones. Then sin entered him, and he coveted the place of the highest God and wanted to be worshipped. Consequently, he was cast down to the earth, where he has since been awaiting damnation: an eternity in the realm of the dead called hell. Unlike Adam and Eve, who were tempted, Satan was not. Rather, his beauty and splendor corrupted him (28:17) and led him to desire to be praised and worshipped.

Unfortunately, the unexpected struck him; God punished him for his sin and destined him to spend eternity into the lake of fire. In response, Satan became defiant, arrogant, and full of hatred toward his Creator and was determined not to perish alone but to drag as many people with him to hell as possible. Swearing to sabotage God's work and his plans for humanity, he led the first couple into sin and is still at work today, driving people away from God using all sorts of schemes to deceive the whole world. To succeed in his plan, he masquerades as an angel of light (2 Cor. 11:14). In other words, he is a usurper, pretending to be something he is not. Ephesians 2:2 portrays him as "a deceiver, a liar, a murderer, an accuser of brethren, a tempter, the prince of the power of air, and the evil one."

Satan is audacious, zealous, and fearless. Why would he fear? His fate is sealed with no room for redemption. He dared to tempt even Jesus, who not only is the Son of the highest God but is also God himself. John, the apostle of Jesus, identified him as the Word that became flesh (John 1:14) and who was present from the beginning of creation.

> "In the beginning was the Word, and the Word was with God, and the Word was God. He was with God in the beginning. Through him all things were made; without him nothing was made that has been made." (1:1–3)

After Jesus fasted for forty days and nights, Satan tried to seduce him into sin using his deceitful tongue. Talking to the One who owns everything, he claimed to own "all kingdoms of the world" and offered, "I will give you all their authority and splendor; it has been given to me, and I can give it to anyone I want to" (Luke 4:5–7). Then asked Jesus, his God, to do the unthinkable: to submit and bow down before him. "If you worship me, it will all be yours," he says (4:7). Who gave Satan such daring and courage? When? Where? Imagine your child coming to you one day and promising to provide you with whatever you want in return for your worship!

People who lust for fame, money, prestige, and success by any means are easy prey to the devil. But although Satan knows the scripture very well (and even quoted it when he tempted Jesus), he is not that smart and lacks true wisdom. Despite the facade presented by his zeal and courage, Satan is, in fact, the stupidest creature that ever existed. He is doomed and can do nothing about it. After the crucifixion of Jesus, Satan thought he had won the battle, but he had only granted Jesus a more incredible victory. As Jesus says, "I am the Living One; I was dead, and now look, I am alive forever and ever! And I hold the keys of death and Hades" (Rev. 1:18).

Jesus rendered Satan powerless because once Jesus took the keys of Hades from him, he could lock up that old serpent anytime he wanted to, and that time is coming soon. After the war of Armageddon, Satan, the beast, and the false prophet will be locked up for a thousand years, as John sees in his vision of the end times:

> "And I saw an angel coming down out of heaven, having the key to the Abyss and holding in his hand a great chain. He seized the dragon, that ancient serpent, who is the devil, or Satan, and bound him for a thousand years. He threw him into the Abyss, and locked and sealed it over him, to keep him from deceiving the nations anymore until the thousand years were ended. After that, he must be set free for a short time." (Rev. 20:1)

Although they will be released briefly after the thousand years, Jesus will then throw them into the lake of fire for eternity.

Another folly of the devil that needs to be highlighted is that his punishment is set and will be implemented when the last believer's life has been given to Christ. After that, the rest of the people's hearts will be inclined to listen to the devil's lies, and wickedness on earth will be at its peak. If he had understood that he was only digging a pit under his own feet and would inevitably fall into it, maybe he would have slowed down or even quit deceiving people to save his own life or at least to delay his punishment. Unfortunately, God has not only sealed Satan's fate but has also deprived him of the capacity to reason. Satan is raging war against God but ultimately knows well that victory is out of his reach. His only consolation is in the number of people he will drag with him to hell. In this regard, we can say that he has been marking some points. Jesus, preaching repentance, called people in to "enter through the narrow gate. For wide is the gate and broad is the road that leads to destruction, and many enter through it" (Matt. 7:13). Unlike humans, to whom God allowed repenting from their sins through Jesus Christ, their Savior, Satan does not have that luxury and privilege. There is no redemption plan for him. After all, he was never tempted: his pride led to his fall.

If Satan was so zealous to tempt even God himself, how much more about you and me? We need to watch out and be alert. Jesus asked his disciples to pray day and night without ceasing. The devil is at work looking for whom to devour and destroy. Early in my journey with Christ, I did not comprehend that call to endless prayers, but the more I grew in faith, the more I understood. Truth be told, Satan does not go after those who are idle in their faith or unbelievers. This class of people already belongs to him and are easily led astray by their own evil desires. It is when someone tries to walk a godly life through Jesus that a tsunami of temptations falls their way. Therefore, believers struggle in life and often feel that unbelievers find more success. Thank God believers can be comforted by the knowledge that a reward awaits them after death.

So, Satan is at work trying to discourage believers and kill faith on earth. Since the beginning of time, God has put into human hearts the desire and longing to worship him, but Satan stepped in and corrupted humans to meet those needs by worshiping false gods. For ages, human beings have replaced true worship with idols in all forms and shapes. And for those who have been smart enough to understand that handmade gods are dead gods, Satan has been driving them into a new form of idolatry, which is the love for money and materials.

Moreover, some Protestant believers adhere to set up a manger in which they put a little wooden "Jesus" at Christmas. I have also noticed that some worship studios, even those built by Protestant denominations, carry drawings of what they call "the Lord" on the windows, and whenever the name of the Lord is mentioned during church services broadcast on TV, the camera operator turns the camera to draw the viewers' attention to those handmade images of god. This is just an attempt for men to fathom and control the god they worship, putting themselves above or making themselves masters of the thing they claim to be their god, their creator, and their provider. What a scandalous way to belittle the God of the universe, the Creator of all things, the God David describes as so humongous that even the heavens cannot contain him. What a shame!

Chapter 7 collects passages from Exodus to Revelation that mention and criticize idol worship. These passages will shed light on the true nature of worship. Let those that have ears understand. I pray that by the time readers get to Revelation, they grasp the magnitude of the living and true God's disappointment to see his beloved children abandon him for useless gods made of wood and iron—gods that do not have eyes to see, ears to understand prayers, or mouths to communicate with their worshippers. God has instructed the Israelites against idols worship using these words:

> "They say to wood, 'You are my father,' and to stone, 'You gave me birth.'
> They have turned their backs to me and not their faces;
> yet when they are in trouble, they say, 'Come and save us!'
> Where then are the gods you made for yourselves?
> Let them come if they can save you when you are in trouble!
> For you, Judah, have as many gods as you have towns" (Jer. 2: 27-28).

They cannot think or walk, yet they have stolen the hearts of people who are so devoted to them that they waste their time, money, and energy in service to them. These gods fit in their pockets, purses, and suitcases to journey with them; they sit in the corners of houses and hang on walls.

Can these people not understand that they own the idols and not the other way around? For owners can do whatever they want with these carved objects. They can put it in a clean or dirty house; they can put it on top of a mountain today and at the bottom of a valley tomorrow, and it will never complain. If they drop it while hiking and come back two months later, they will find it lying right where it was dropped, unless someone else has picked it up or the rain or wind has carried it away. If a god cannot do anything for itself, how will it do anything for them?

Stressing on these foolish practices, The Lord declares:

> "Behind your doors and your doorposts,
>   you have put your pagan symbols…
> When you cry out for help, let your collection of
> idols save you!
>   The wind will carry all of them off; a mere
>   breath will blow them away.
> But whoever takes refuge in me will inherit the land
>   and possess my holy mountain" (Is. 57: 8, 13).

Let us see what the living God, the one and only true God, can do for himself. When David attempted to bring the ark of the living God back to Jerusalem, he transported it in an unworthy manner, having it pulled along in a cart rather than carried in the manner God had instructed.

"When they came to the threshing floor of Kidon, Uzzah reached out his hand to steady the ark, because the oxen stumbled. The Lord's anger burned against Uzzah, and he struck him down because he had put his hand on the ark. So, he died there before God. Then David was angry because the Lord's wrath had broken out against Uzzah, and to this day that place is called Perez Uzzah. David was afraid of God that day and asked, "How can I ever bring the ark of God to me?" He did not take the ark to be with him in the City of David. Instead, he took it to the house of Obed-Edom the Gittite. The ark of God remained with the family of Obed-Edom in his house for three months, and the Lord blessed his household and everything he had" . (1 Chron. 13:9–14)

Now *this* is a God who can do great things. Amen!

As stated above, idol worshippers fit their handmade gods into their luggage to travel or put it in corners of their homes, and it will stay in place forever until anybody decides to move it to another location. How can a house contain a god? Why do people belittle their gods and shame them, elevating themselves above the gods they worship? While they get first-class tickets for themselves, they let their gods travel locked up in suitcases. While they live in comfortable homes, they leave their gods outside in their front yards, scorching in the summer sun or cracking in the winter cold.

In contrast, King David describes the immensity of the almighty and living God, asking, "who is able to build a temple for him, since the heavens, even the highest heavens, cannot contain him? Who then am I to build a temple for him, except as a place to burn sacrifices before him?" (2 Chron. 2:6) David also foresaw the greatness of God and commanded the heads of gates and doors to be lifted up so that the king of glory might enter, for they were too small for the great God that he is (Ps. 24:7).

Why do people work so hard to find out what God might look like? This is what leads to idolatry. The true God declares that a sinful person cannot see him face to face, or they will die. After communicating verbally with God for a long time in the tent of meeting, Moses pleaded, "Now show me your glory" (Ex. 33:18). However, God refused, arranging instead to let Moses see his glory as he passed by.

> "And the Lord said, "I will cause all my goodness to pass in front of you, and I will proclaim my name, the Lord, in your presence. I will have mercy on whom I will have mercy, and I will have compassion on whom I will have compas-sion. But," he said, "you cannot see my face, for no one may see me and live." Then the Lord said, "There is a place near me where you may stand on a rock. When my glory passes by, I will put you in a cleft in the rock and cover you with my hand until I have passed by. Then I will

remove my hand and you will see my back; but my face must not be seen." (33:19–23)

For this reason, Moses commanded the sons and daughters of Israel never to cast an idol or worship it. He reminded them of a time when the living God had spoken to them:

> "You saw no form of any kind the day the Lord spoke to you at Horeb out of the fire. Therefore watch yourselves very carefully, so that you do not become corrupt and make for yourselves an idol, an image of any shape, whether formed like a man or a woman, or like any animal on earth or any bird that flies in the air, or like any creature that moves along the ground or any fish in the waters below. And when you look up to the sky and see the sun, the moon and the stars—all the heavenly array—do not be enticed into bowing down to them and worshiping things the Lord your God has apportioned to all the nations under heaven. But as for you, the Lord took you and brought you out of the iron-smelting furnace, out of Egypt, to be the people of his inheritance, as you now are." (Deut. 4:15–20)

It is a shame that despite God's stern warning, people have been so defiant and careless. God—who once said Moses would die if he saw God's face—is the same yesterday, today, and tomorrow. Trying to represent him on a sheet of paper or with any other kind of art is sickening and ludicrous because people are trying to give him an image that is not his. No one has ever seen him face to face.

I know people will argue that Jesus was seen while on earth, but they ought to remember that he was also there every time God stated all over the Bible that humans should not carve stone or worship it. Jesus did not come to do away with "the Law or the Prophets," he says. He continues,

> "I have not come to abolish them but to fulfill them. For truly I tell you, until heaven and earth disappear, not the smallest letter, not the least stroke of a pen, will by any means disappear from the Law until everything is accomplished. Therefore, anyone who sets aside one of the least of these commands and teaches others accordingly will be called least in the kingdom of heaven, but whoever practices and teaches these commands will be called great in the kingdom of heaven." (Matt. 5:17–19)

After his resurrection, the Bible recounts that Jesus appeared to two of his disciples on the road to Emmaus, and they did not recognize him until he took the veil off their eyes during their meal.

> "When he was at the table with them, he took bread, gave thanks, broke it and began to give

it to them. Then their eyes were opened, and they recognized him, and he disappeared from their sight. They asked each other, "Were not our hearts burning within us while he talked with us on the road and opened the Scriptures to us?" (Luke 24:30–32)

Why then would we carve images of him anyway? Whose face is it that idol worshippers attribute to Jesus? Even the people who walked with him for more than three years did not recognize him after his resurrection.

The representation of Jesus as seen today is very similar to that of Nimrod, carved thousands of years before Jesus Christ was born. Hislop stressed that the circle on the head on the carved image of Jesus was found as well on the image of the Roman Madonna and on the head of Apollo(87).

When Isaiah, the prophet, was transported to heaven by the Holy Spirit and saw the face of the Almighty, he knew he was going to die and deplored his fate. Fortunately, his sin was atoned right there to save his life.

> "Woe to me!" I cried. "I am ruined! For I am a man of unclean lips, and I live among a people of unclean lips, and my eyes have seen the King, the Lord Almighty."
>
> Then one of the seraphim flew to me with a live coal in his hand, which he had taken with tongs from the altar. With it he touched my mouth

and said, "See, this has touched your lips; your guilt is taken away and your sin atoned for." (Isa. 6:5–7)

God himself had brought him there to assign him the mission of turning his chosen ones away from sin and idol worship, so Isaiah was spared. However, even the seraphim—the angelic beings who dwell in the presence of the Almighty, praising him days and nights—are not allowed to see God face to face; instead, "with two wings they cover their faces, and with two they covered their feet" in the presence of the living God (6:2).

Why should a sinful man seek the face of a holy God? That should not happen. Only the elect, born-again Christians, those who have washed their clothes in the Lamb's blood, will see God face to face when God himself descends from heaven. Bringing with him the new Jerusalem, he will dwell among his people, his children, for eternity, when time will be no more. At that time, "no longer will there be any curse. The throne of God and the Lamb will be in the city, and his servants will serve him. They will see his face, and his name will be on their foreheads" (Rev. 22:3–4). Amen.

The devil is a liar. Do not let him fool you into seeking the face of God. God is too holy, too beautiful, too great, too magnificent to fit on your necklaces, in your pockets and wallets, or on your walls and porches. Let those that have ears understand.

While waiting for the return of Jesus Christ, the Apostle Paul commanded Timothy (and us) to follow God's commands "without spot or blame until the appearing of our Lord Jesus

Christ, which God will bring about in his own time—God, the blessed and only Ruler, the King of kings, Lord of lords, and the God of gods, who alone is immortal and who lives in unapproachable light, whom no one has seen or can see. To him be honor and might forever. Amen" (1 Tim. 6:14–16).

I should also mention that beside carved images of Jesus (or should I say Nimrod) and Mary (Semiramis), Catholics also worship communion, a practice that is modeled nowhere in the Bible. On Good Fridays in my church in Cameroon, a special, grand communion would be set apart in a beautiful trophy like vase, and people all day long would kneel before it and pray. I remember the last time I participated; I tried and failed to pray before that piece of unleavened bread for about five minutes. My God was already speaking to me in a special way. Then, for the first time, I finally felt and grasped the foolishness of talking to a piece of bread. I ran away. Thank you, Jesus.

Remember, Lord, that your children are still losing their minds in that church of Nimrod. The pope teaches that the communion bread, baked in an oven, is truly the body of Christ and that the wine, made in a vineyard cellar, has been supernaturally changed into the blood of Christ. They bring their votaries to kneel and worship that bread and wine, but when does that transformation process take place? At harvest in the wheat farms and vineyards? In the factories where grains and grapes are changed into flour and wine? When the dough is mixed up with olive oil, or when it comes out of the oven? Is it when the portion purchased for the purpose of Eucharist reaches Catholic soil? Or is it when the priest lifts it up and murmurs a prayer that Jesus descends miraculously and inhabits the bread and wine? This is nothing but dumb belief.

Forty days after his resurrection, Jesus went up to heaven and promised to return in the end times. Does the Jesus that the Catholic Church worship descend from heaven for every Mass ceremony and instill himself into communion elements so that its votaries can eat his flesh and drink his blood? While still on earth and even in his physical body, Jesus instituted the Passover meal and ate it too. His blood was still running down and up within his physical body. Therefore, what he instituted was nothing but a symbol to remember his life and suffering and the gift of life birthed. The first disciples who took part in the first Passover meal did not eat and drink the true flesh and blood of Jesus, for he was there at their side. If his physical flesh and blood were to be used, Jesus would not have needed to die on the cross. His disciples could have butchered him right there and partaken of his flesh and blood, or they could have taken his body from the cross after his death to perform the sacrament.

When Jesus first preached the eating of his flesh and drinking of his blood to his disciples all gathered, some of them thought (like Catholics) that he was speaking literally.

> "Jesus said to them, "Very truly I tell you, unless you eat the flesh of the Son of Man and drink his blood, you have no life in you. Whoever eats my flesh and drinks my blood has eternal life, and I will raise them up at the last day. For my flesh is real food and my blood is real drink.

Whoever eats my flesh and drinks my blood remains in me, and I in them. Just as the living Father sent me and I live because of the Father, so the one who feeds on me will live because of me. This is the bread that came down from heaven. Your ancestors ate manna and died, but whoever feeds on this bread will live forever. On hearing it, many of his disciples said, "This is a hard teaching. Who can accept it? From this time many of his disciples turned back and no longer followed him". (John 6:53–58, 60, 66)

They were smarter than Catholic votaries to have run away. Eating real flesh and blood would be purely satanic.

What did Jesus mean by those words? In his first epistle, John again presents Jesus as the Word that was made flesh and dwelt among men. Therefore, the flesh Jesus talks about is nothing but the Word of God, and he was calling people to study it. How else would you know about him, his precepts, and his requirements? My dear Catholic votaries, you have been fooled for so long. It is time to open your eyes and see. In the Name of Jesus, Amen! This is simply another form of idolatry, for the symbolic Passover meal has been turned into an object of worship in and of itself.

Similarly, in the Old Testament, the judge, Gideon, collected the gold the Israelites had plundered from the Ishmaelites—1,700 shekels' worth—and he turned it into an ephod. Unfortunately, although it was meant to be an instrument of worship, the Israelites worshipped the ephod itself and "prostituted themselves by worshiping it there, and it became a snare to Gideon and his family" (Judg. 8:27). Even the bronze snake Moses had once made at God's command—which God had used to cure the Israelites of the bites of poisonous snakes in the wilderness—had to be broken into pieces by King Ahaz of Judah because the Jews were burning incense to it. King Ahaz's action was credited to him as righteousness (2 Kings 17:4).

The perfect description of Roman Catholic Church is found in 2 Kings 17:9–41 (see chapter 7, part 10 of this book), a passage in which God undresses the Catholic Church and exposes their deeds through another account of idolatry. Through many prophets and for many years, the almighty, true God had warned the Israelites against idol worship, but because they did not listen, God rejected them and allowed them to be taken captive by Assyria. The Assyrian king allied his kingdom with the nations of Babylon, Avva, Hamath, and Sepharvaim to occupy the emptied land of Samaria. These new occupants were taught the ways of the Lord, which they received joyfully; however, though "they worshiped the Lord…they also served their own gods in accordance with the customs of the nations from which they had been brought" (17:33). "Even while these people were worshiping the Lord, they were serving their idols. To this day, their children and grandchildren continue to do as their ancestors did" (17:41).

This is a crystal-clear image of the Roman Catholic Church. The Apostle Paul warned against false doctrines from false apostles, saying,

> "But I am afraid that just as Eve was deceived by the serpent's cunning, your minds may somehow be led astray from your sincere and pure devotion to Christ. For if someone comes to you and preaches a Jesus other than the Jesus we preached, or if you receive a different spirit from the Spirit you received, or a different gospel from the one you accepted, you put up with it easily enough." (2 Cor. 11:3–4)

Even at the beginning of Christianity, Satan was already infiltrating false teachers into the early church in order to sabotage the mighty work of Jesus Christ. Paul identifies the presence of "false apostles, deceitful workers, masquerading as apostles of Christ. And no wonder, for Satan himself masquerades as an angel of light. It is not surprising, then, if his servants also masquerade as servants of righteousness" (11:13–15). Paul was distressed by effects of these false teachers, saying in his letter to the Galatians,

> "I am astonished that you are so quickly deserting the one who called you to live in the grace of Christ and are turning to a different gospel—which is really no gospel at all. Evidently some people are throwing you into confusion and are trying to pervert the gospel of Christ. But even if we or an angel from heaven should preach a gospel other than the one we preached to you, let them be under God's curse!" (Gal. 1:6–9)

There is only one true gospel, Paul warns emphatically.

Aside from promoting idolatry, the Roman Catholic Church also misleads people by forbidding priests from marrying. That is not the gospel of Jesus. The vow of celibacy has become a trap and a stumbling block for Catholic priests. The burden imposed on them by the Vatican pushes them into gay relationships and into vicious pedophilia, destroying the lives of innocent children. Paul warned against this specific rule in 1 Timothy 4:1–3 two thousand years ago: "The Spirit clearly says that in later times some will abandon the faith and follow deceiving spirits and things taught by demons. Such teachings come through hypocritical liars, whose consciences have been seared as with a hot iron. They forbid people to marry."

Let those that have ears understand.

CHAPTER 4

My Personal Experience—from Idol Worshipper to Born-Again Christian

My Catholic heritage came from my family. My mom was a devoted Catholic idol worshipper. In her early walk, she invested most of her time carrying on many church activities, including conducting the choir. As we grew up, juggling family and church responsibilities became quite tricky, so she held back and reserved herself mostly to attending church on Sundays. As far as our faith was concerned, we children walked in our mom's shoes and were baptized and confirmed Catholic.

A fantastic story is that of my older sister, who quit going to church for a long time amid personal struggles and difficulties. When she was ready to go back to church, she wasn't sure which one to choose because her husband was Protestant. Reluctant and hesitant, she asked God for a sign to help her make the right choice, and he led her into the Protestant church. As I was still Catholic, I was profoundly shocked and hurt that she would make such a choice.

We are Catholics and should die as Catholics, I remember murmuring. However, couldn't do anything about it.

After my own experience being born-again, I decided to write a testimony and share it with the clergy of my former church, and it is as follows.

Testimony [translated from French]

Dear Sir Jean-Marie Signe,

I praise the Lord for allowing me to have your address. I take this opportunity to send you my warm greetings. The primary purpose of this letter is to testify about my Christian life. These are things that have particularly marked and transformed me to make me a new creature. Here is my story. It is a bit long, but I pray that God gives you time to read it all:

I come from a Catholic "Christian" family and have been a devout follower of this religion for many years. Only God can testify exactly how many times I swore never to leave the Catholic Church. I always did it under the pressure of Protestant Christians who told me, "You Catholics worship idols and Mary." My prompt response every time was, "That's false. You only desire to drag me out of my beloved Catholic church. Let me tell you something: it will never happen. Trust me; I am Catholic, and I will remain and die Catholic."

That's right. I had never been against other religious denominations. And one thing I was sure of was that my path led me to Christ. I remember at Elig-Essono High School, I had classmates who were from Protestant denominations, and one of them preached to me on a regular basis, mostly talking about the new birth.

He regularly asked me the following question: "Are you converted? Are you born again?" He then explained, "He who is converted is born again."

I obviously answered him, "Yes, I am."

Then he continued, "When did you convert?"

"I cannot give you a date, but I know that I am converted. I believe in God," I replied.

"Without any offense, allow me to tell you that you are not transformed by the Holy Spirit yet; you are not born again. If that were the case, you would know the date—because it's a special day that you will never forget—or you would at least remember the circumstances!"

"Be clearer," I replied.

"There are particular signs that authenticate your conversion, which stick in your mind forever; a truly converted person cannot forget that wonderful day of their life." He also told me exactly when he had received the Lord.

That day he had brought with him one of his sisters in Christ, and amazingly both used similar words to speak about conversion accompanied by signs. I was very surprised to hear them speak with such assurance, with such zeal.

I simply told them, "I've never had any sign, but I'm sure of one thing: I'm a Christian, and I love God with all my heart. I think that's enough for me."

"What denomination are you in?" they asked me.

"That's where you were heading; I knew it. I am Catholic."

"So, you love the statues and Mary—"

"I do not worship a statue, and I will never do it," I replied. [That answer was nothing but a big fat lie, and it constitutes a major stumbling block for Catholics].

"Yes, you do. If you want to be converted, if you want to receive the signs that we are talking about, go home and confess your sins. The Lord will manifest himself to you."

"Every day in my prayer, I do not forget to confess my sins," I replied.

"And you have never seen a sign?" he asked me.

"No. Never."

"That's because you did not recollect them all. You omitted some. Tonight, start it all over again. Try to recall all your sins, if possible. Make sure to write them down on a sheet of paper to remember them all during your prayer session, and shun omitting anything," the guy told me.

"It's crazy what you ask me. How can someone recall all their sins—stuff that happened many years ago? It's impossible."

"It is possible indeed! I recollected all of mine and confessed them all," he insisted with great assurance. "If you put in a little time, with the help of God, you'll get there."

Back home, I searched my past for all mistakes and errors I had committed voluntarily or involuntarily—at least those which I could still remember. I wrote them down and was sure that the list was not exhaustive. It had about five or six things I could remember so far, and I confessed them anyway. How hard is it for somebody to identify their faults and mistakes? I remember asking God that day to forgive me for even what I could not remember, but I still did not receive any sign. What was wrong? I could not answer that question, but I thought that maybe God chose those to whom he would give the signs, or that it was imperative to quote every single mistake done in the past. But how could I do that?

My dear classmate kept bugging me with the same question throughout the year: Have you received any sign yet? The answer each time was obviously no. Curiously, every time he questioned me, he invited me to go back to the confession closet. And sure enough, on those evenings, I would repeat my confession, but I never received any signs. In the end, I felt tired of these inquiries and unfruitful recurrent confessions. I always said to myself that all they wanted was to get me out of the Catholic Church, but that would not happen. I was Catholic, and I would die Catholic. [If you are a Catholic reading this note, do you ever remember quoting these same words to somebody trying to preach to you? Without a shadow of doubt, I can answer for you, and that answer is, "Yes, you have."

Why is it that Catholics do not have the flexibility of spirit and mind to open themselves to any other messages than those they receive in their so-called Mass? It looks like the same spirit is controlling them. Why, then, do they all seal their faith by proclaiming that they will live and die as Catholics? In Africa, you hear the same lyric; in Europe, the same song, and the United States. I have never been to Asia, but would it be any different there?]

The end of the academic year came and freed me from my classmates. Yeah!

My daily life was far from being a happy life. It was marked by things that made me immensely sad. One of those things was nightmares. Very often, I had nightmares, basically about a deluge—destruction by water and fire. The things I saw in those nightmares did not vary too much. The place could vary, but the common point was the destruction in which men perished by fire and flood. I will briefly mention a few:

In Yaounde, in one of my nightmares, I found myself in a neighborhood crowded with peo-ple, and suddenly, fire sprang up, threatening to encircle the whole district and its inhabitants. A general panic ensued. Everyone was trying to find a way out. I struggled as best as I could, and that day, luck smiled on me. Just when I came out of town with three or four other people, the fire surrounded the city and all its inhabitants.

In another, I was in a house with people I did not know, and the lava surprised us; there was no way out for anyone.

In another one, I was in the middle of a field lined with big, medium, and small snakes. Some were so long that I could neither see their heads nor their tails.

I cannot count how many times these nightmares bugged me. Waking up from my sleep was always a great relief because it released me from those dark and tragic episodes.

I thought I had left my nightmares behind me in Germany, but they followed me everywhere I had to go. The scenario was always the same: fire or flood. I remember praying in Germany several times for the Lord to deliver me from them. Curiously, the more I prayed, the more frequently I had them—like about once a week.

Sometimes, it was my village neighborhood that was targeted, especially our family home. Several times in my nightmares, I saw our property go up in smoke. The dream that particularly shocked me was the one in which we could not save my little brother. The rest of the family ran away to safety. However, he tried to escape through the roof and unfortunately was trapped, and from a distance, we watched him perish in flames.

It was difficult to bear. I could not stand it anymore, and I kept praying that God would end this form of torture. Then, one night in March 2001, I had the last nightmare of that magnitude:

We were three people, and I knew neither where we were going nor who they were. On arriving at one place, one of us took a shovel and started digging up a small tree. I could not identify what kind of tree it was. Solving that puzzle wasn't of great importance. Around the tree, he made a square and dug down. As he was still digging, I noticed something rolled around the roots and called his attention to it.

"What could it be?" I asked him.

Without answering, he reached down and touched it. I had the impression that he was trying to find out what it was. Even though I was frightened, the temptation of touching it too was irresistible. Why not? If he had touched it, I could do it also. And sure enough, I reached down and touched it as well. I immediately felt a strange sensation and quickly removed my hand. It had felt very soft and cold. At the same time, I noticed a piece of it coming out of the ground and winding around the tree. I called that person's attention to it one more time and made up my mind to follow it to figure out how far it went. After a few steps, I saw the end of it—I mean, the head of it. I was stunned and petrified. It was the head of a snake.

I shouted out loud, "It's the devil, I touched the devil with my hand. How can God do this to me, letting me touch the devil with my bare hands?"

I couldn't be more scared. For the rest of that episode, I found myself in my bedroom in Germany. It was about 6:00 a.m., and my husband was playing a religious CD. The lyrics were a call to conversion. I had the apprehension that he had put the music on to evangelize me. I rebelled against him, and with rough and extreme anger, I told him to stop the music.

I added, "Every time, you asked me to be converted. How many times have I told you that I am? I'm tired of your reproaches."

Suddenly, I woke up and was in extreme shock. That day, I experienced the greatest fear of my life. I had touched the devil with my hands. What was the meaning of this? I could not keep this nightmare to myself. I was so tormented that I decided to share it with my husband.

He replied, "I have always summoned you to give your life to Christ, and you have never listened to me. I think your dream is a call to conversion."

Then I asked him, "What kind of conversion is it? Because I have recollections of my high school classmates, who invited me on many occasions to confess my sins and be born again. I did it each time I received such a call or inquiry, but I never got the signs they spoke about. Every day, I confess my sins, and I do not see what other form or kind of confession you guys are asking of me."

He answered me, "You never confessed all your sins. I've always told you that Catholics have antibiblical practices, such as worshipping statues, worshipping Mary. I think you should think about it seriously."

After his departure to work, sure enough, I thought about it. Every single individual that had hitherto invited me to repentance had condemned the acts of idolatry that—according to them—were practiced in the Catholic Church. On the other hand, in my multiple attempts at confession, I had never alluded to the act of idolatry. [The only rational explanation for this attitude is that Catholic votaries find themselves locked up in a state of denial. They want to remain in that state forever to avoid the psychologically uncomfortable truth about idols and worship. In my opinion back then, I believed I had never practiced such an act, despite all the clear evidences. Big lie! The devil is a liar. How do you address something that isn't a problem to you at all? Something that you have never considered to be a subject for discussion.]

However, hardening my heart one more time was not an option because I did not want to undergo another nightmare. Therefore, I told God, "if I'm guilty of it, and if that's what will make the list of my sins complete, I'll admit it." I went to the living room with our daughter and confessed it, using these words: "I put behind me the Catholic Church and its idolatrous practices." This was the only sin I confessed that day.

As soon as I uttered these words, I felt the burden of my sins lifted and taken away, and suddenly, I felt so light. I really felt a weight fall away from me, and a profound joy invaded my soul. It would be best if you experienced this to understand the full depth of the joy. I sang, and I praised the Lord. I did not sing alone; the angels sang with me. I felt it. The story of the prodigal son can help you understand a little more. I was that prodigal child lost and found. I realized that Kim—my high school classmate—and his companions had been right.

Since that day, I have not had nightmares of such magnitude. I found a joy of life I did not have before. The urge to read the Bible has become very natural to me now. I do it effortlessly; on the other hand, in the past, at least before the day I was born again, I had a strong will and a burning desire to read the Bible, but I rarely took action. Even when I happened to sit down and open it, I quickly felt idle; something in me kept me from doing it—the devil, certainly.

I understood a lot in a short time. In Jesus Christ, everything is light and easy. Jesus said, "my yoke is easy."

We do not need to do violence to abstain from the things of this world. When others do these things around us, we are just disgusted. Dear Jean Marie, I understood why your efforts to discipline people in Elig-Edzoa were in vain. I saw you acting. I saw in you someone who wanted to see church members testify of their faith by the way they live. Unfortunately, your actions did not bear fruit.

On the contrary, people did not care at all. Sometimes I even felt sorry for you. On the one hand, the church group activities I saw were all that a group could be except Christian. At least the ones I knew, the lives of these people, did not reflect a Christian's life, and nobody made any effort in that direction. They all had the same chorus, "After all, we are humans."

Given all that I observed, I always wondered what was wrong, because, on the other hand, I was also watching the lives of Protestant Christians. If you remember, I told you that everyone I lived with was Protestant. Through this bond, I rubbed shoulders with their brethren in Christ regularly. I saw in them the true meaning of love and care. I saw how they prayed for each other with fervent zeal. The love of neighbor was inked into them. I have a distant cousin on my mother's side with whom I was in Yaoundé. When my mother had an accident, his choir came to pray for her at the University hospital center. The members of my choir did not feel interested. Sophie [one of my friends in our choir group] had the same problem with her dad, and the list is not exhaustive. The only things that unite everyone in Elig-Edzoa are boy-girl friend relationships, gossip, night clubs, and cinema.

The only valid explanation I give to this is the absence of God's true presence because he is greatly displeased with idols and cut images. Even someone who reads the Bible only from Genesis to Joshua cannot doubt this. You will undoubtedly claim like I did, that Catholics do not worship statues; with all due respect, I assure you that you are mistaken. Looking at a sculpture, a carved image, and uttering prayers is nothing but idolatry. Who are you talking too, if not to the object in front of you, the thing you are staring at? An object that does not have eyes to see you, ears to understand, or a mouth to talk. It was to put away these practices that Jesus told the Samaritan lady that a time is coming when true worshippers would worship him in spirit. If it were not the case, I would never have been guilty of it and would not have needed to confess it to earn my born-again certificate.

I remembered bowing down before Mary's statue during a prayer session on one of our choir excursions at the main Catholic Church in Mvolyé, in the place where the statue of Mary stands. However, I couldn't pray that day. I had the feeling I was addressing a mute object, a carved stone, the work of human hands. I truly experienced the feeling I have described, and since then, I decided never to do it again and wondered how people could address a simple polished stone in their prayers.

God was already speaking to me in this way, through the feeling of discomfort when carrying out such an act. Given that these statues are all over the church's place and around it, church members genuinely do not have any choice but to stare at them when they pray. [Before my conversion, at home during my prayers time with God, I let my spirit wander to the church, trying to recapture those images that we call "god" that hang on walls. This was a giant stumbling block after my conversion. Thank God, with time, I dealt with it. Because of this, I hate riding past any Catholic Churches, for fear of accidentally letting my eyes stumble on those useless idols]. Based on my experience, I affirm that the Catholic Church without its statues and idolatrous practices, such as the adoration of the Blessed Sacrament, would make a better church.

There is another practice I would like to denounce here: the holy waters. I have heard several people claiming that they cannot stay at home without holy water. With this water, they feel safe and protected. Does water have a protective power? It is, without the shadow of doubt, another form of idolatry. God makes it clear in his Holy Book that he is a jealous God. Therefore, we incite his anger every time we trust in frivolous objects such as holy water, statues, and rosaries instead of trusting in him, our Savior.

God hates idolatrous practices. I noticed it when I went through the books of the Pentateuch.

He warns the Jews several times against any covenant with the inhabitants of the land they would enter, lest they be corrupted by them and bow down to their idols.

Exodus 23:32: "Do not make a covenant with them or with their gods."

Similarly, Exodus 34:12–14: "Be careful not to make a treaty with those who live in the land where you are going, or they will be a snare among you. Break down their altars, smash their sacred stones and cut down their Asherah poles. Do not worship any other god, for the LORD, whose name is Jealous, is a jealous God."

Exodus 34:17: "Do not make any idols."

Numbers 33:52: "drive out all the inhabitants of the land before you. Destroy all their carved images and their cast idols and demolish all their high places."

Deuteronomy 7:5: "This is what you are to do to them: Break down their altars, smash their sacred stones, cut down their Asherah poles and burn their idols in the fire."

Deuteronomy 12:3: "Break down their altars, smash their sacred stones and burn their Asherah poles in the fire; cut down the idols of their gods and wipe out their names from those places."

Deuteronomy 16:21–22: "Do not set up any wooden Asherah pole beside the altar you build to the LORD your God, and do not erect a sacred stone, for these the LORD your God hates."

John 4:23–24: "Yet a time is coming and has now come when the true worshipers will worship the Father in the Spirit and in truth, for they are the kind of worshipers the Father seeks. God is spirit, and his worshipers must worship in the Spirit and in truth."

God is therefore Spirit and not a cut stone. A man does not know what his own spirit looks like. How could he possibly represent God (who is Spirit) in these conditions?

Why does man want to fashion his own god? What is the definition of God? Whoever manufactures or buys an object (like a statue or a cut stone) is the Master of It. How, then, does man prostrate himself before his own work?

In Leviticus, God promises curses to all who violate his ordinances. And God repeatedly insists in his law against the act of idolatry: "Do not make idols or set up an image or a sacred stone for yourselves, and do not place a carved stone in your land to bow down before it. I am the Lord your God" (Lev. 26:1).

In the Psalms, King David states, "All who worship images are put to shame, those who boast in idols— worship him, all you gods!" (Ps. 97:7).

The list is far from exhaustive. If God insists so strongly against idolatry and repeats himself so many times, it is because he hates it. Let us not forget that he is a jealous God who visits the iniquity of fathers on children until the third and fourth generation (Deut. 5:9).

I invite you, dear Jean-Marie, to ask God for signs. Let him show you the way forward. The way of carved images is not good, I'm sure. I beg you not to harden your heart like I had done for so long. I remembered having longed several times, when my friends would speak badly about the Catholic Church, to ask God for signs that would lead me to the right path by following my sister's steps. However, something in me prevented me from doing so. I was afraid that the truth about God was something other than what I aspired to. I have never longed to quit the Catholic Church and wondered in my heart what I would do if, by asking for signs, God ever directed me to a Protestant church. I whispered in my heart, "No, I do not want to leave the Catholic Church" or "Do not do that. Do not ask for any sign."

That was a whisper from the devil.

Fortunately, God used nightmares to snatch me out of that slimy pit. What a wonderful God we serve! Now I realize that my faith was solely based on the church denomination, on the church as a building and not on Jesus Christ.

I give thanks to God because he extends his hand to those who seek him with all their hearts, for he says in Jeremiah 29:13–14, "You will seek me and find me when you seek me with all your heart. I will be found by you," declares the LORD"

Moreover, the ways of the Lord are unfathomable. I give thanks to the Lord, and I can never thank him enough for this precious gift. He put me among his elect. I beg you once more not to harden your heart but to ask God to help you. I am sure that he will show you the way that leads to him if you do so. It is the most important part; the rest is vanity and worse, and it takes us away from Jesus.

May the Lord bless you and give you a lucid mind so that you may say, like Nebuchadnezzar, "At the end of that time, I, Nebuchadnezzar, raised my eyes toward heaven, and my sanity was restored. Then I praised the Most High; I honored and glorified him who lives forever" (Dan. 4:34).

Umeå on 17/07/2003

Ernestine Désirée Kouokam

CHAPTER 5

Should Christians Celebrate the End-of-Year Festivals?

Christmas

IT ALWAYS AMAZES ME THAT parents, in their passion for Christmas, use the myth of Santa Claus to celebrate the event. They pierce their little ones' souls with lies and masquerade it in some pretentious fun and amusement. Yes, Santa Claus will get you whatever you want for Christmas, sliding down the chimney on Christmas Eve and depositing your gift under the tree, and you'll have it when you get up on Christmas Day. The myth of Santa Claus borrowed its belief from pagans' end of year celebrations before Christianity.

In Scandinavian mythology, Julebuk is believed to be the god "Woden." He paid a visit to each home during the holiday wearing a scary horned mask, but he would share presents with kids despite his monster's look. Another goddess, "Berchta", is also described as riding a pale horse, randomly bringing blessings and curses to people (Flynn, 48). Therefore, people waited for her with fear, not knowing whether they would receive a blessing or a curse. In order "to influence her decision, a meal of fish and dumplings would be left out, and there would also be a serving of oats for her horse" (48).

Even though the Santa Claus myth lines up with that of Woden, it has evolved with time. While Woden's arrival is presented as scary, that of Santa Claus has been cleaned from filth and flaws and is presented on a golden platter with only good stuff. That is why poor children are so excited at Christmas's approach, not knowing that Santa Claus is just a fable and a pure lie put forth by the system and employed by parents to manipulate and pierce their little souls. For parents, it might sound funny at first; however, when time comes for a reality check, it becomes a great challenge. Parents find it extremely difficult to transition from the lie to the truth about Santa without hurting their children's feelings. This cultural lie has been so anchored into people's lives that it has become normal. Articles are written—not advising people to tell the truth to their kids—but educating them on making that transition less painful. Why not avoiding creating the problem in the first place? Is it really the birth of Jesus that people celebrate at Christmas?

Jesus declared in John 14:6, "I am the way and the truth and the life." Why do people use lies to celebrate a God whose attribute is truth? Yet the tradition of Santa Claus has been anchored into people's minds and souls and grafted into the rituals of Christmas celebrations to the point where it is generally accepted. While Christmas is not universally accepted, it is still surprisingly celebrated virtually everywhere. Pagans and Christians share the same decorations and practices for the event. Yet in some of those pagan nations, some Christians are being persecuted and killed for their faith. History shows that Christmas borrows its origin from pagan religions, and because of the reality and fascinating stories about the birth of Jesus Christ, Christians have embraced that festivity with all its flaws and dirt, caring solely about the person of Jesus, to whom all glory and honor should be given. In other words, Christians think it is okay for them to adopt non-Christian rituals as long as they say it is about Jesus.

I have sought and discovered how Christmas originated and how it has transitioned into Christian faith and worship. Let's go back to Hislop's fascinating discovery, which has been overlooked by churches for ages. Most Christian in the Western world now knows for sure that Jesus could not have been born on the twenty-fifth of December, given the climatic challenges the shepherds would have encountered. However, in the equatorial region, where people never experience winter, it is considered a reality and an unchallenged truth that Jesus was born on the twenty-fifth of December, unless people from this region have received some religious insight or have been lucky enough to be told the truth about Christmas.

I was shocked the day I learned that Jesus wasn't born on that specific day. What? The truth about Jesus's birthday was so deeply anchored in my soul that I could only be shocked when the news vibrated into my ears. It is nothing else but a pure lie, and Christians are using lies to celebrate a God of Truth. Yet it is by the attribute of truth that Jesus distinguishes himself from the devil, whom he describes as "a murderer from the beginning, not holding to the truth, for there is no truth in him. When he lies, he speaks his native language, for he is a liar and the father of lies" (John 8:44). Even if Christians decide to separate Christmas from the twenty-fifth of December—which I believe to be a better deal, but unless you have the actual date of Jesus's birth—it will remain a pure lie.

But the Bible is silent about the date of Jesus's birth, mainly because had Jesus not died on the cross to atone for the sin of humankind, his journey on earth would have been just like anybody else's life. It is his work on the cross—not his birth—that sets him apart from the crowd, and that lifts him up as the Savior of the world. And it is his death and resurrection that he expressly required to be commemorated:

> "After taking the cup, he gave thanks and said, "Take this and divide it among you. For I tell you I will not drink again from the fruit of the vine until the kingdom of God comes." And he took bread, gave thanks and broke it, and gave it to them, saying, "This is my body given for you; do this in remembrance of me." In the same way, after the supper he took the cup, saying, "This cup is the new covenant in my blood, which is poured out for you." (Luke 22:17–20)

Why do people invest themselves so much in such a controversial celebration as Christmas? Before I elaborate on Christmas's origin, let's talk about what must occur before birth: conception. In the Bible, the conception of Jesus is portrayed as the fruit of the holy spirit, which surpasses human perception and understanding. The Holy Spirit visited the Virgin Mary, and she conceived her son. The Catholic denomination has selected March 25, called "Lady Day," to celebrate the miraculous conception. However, the Bible does not allude to any date as the time of Jesus's conception (Hislop, 102). This is just another extra event observed by Catholics that is not required by God.

Why do they emphasize Jesus's conception? Remember that worshippers of Semiramis also boldly proclaimed that she miraculously conceived her son. In fact, according to Hislop, the March 25 was a day "observed in pagan Rome in honor of Cybele, the mother of the Babylonian messiah" (102). Furthermore, his findings have proven that "December 25 was, in fact, the birth[day] of the son of the Babylonian queen of heaven" (93). The time from March 25 to December 25 is a full gestational period, but if Nimrod was conceived on March 25 and born on December 25, Hislop wonders what chances there are that the true Messiah's conception and birth would follow the exact same pattern (102).

Nimrod was the star of his time; while alive, he was admired, trusted, venerated, and looked upon with awe by his followers. They loved him with passion. No wonder his death for them was a disaster and a significant loss. His adepts did all they could to keep his spirit alive, so they likely commemorated his birth long after his death. In quest of members in the third century, the Roman Catholic Church adopted Nimrod's birthday festival and just changed its name into "Christmas."

Everything else about the festival and traditions remained the same (Hislop, 93). For example, the Babylonians also used candles to exalt their god, and they lit his altar with them (97). Moreover, the Christmas tree, which has nowadays become "mandatory" in the celebration of Christmas, was used in the primitive Roman and Egyptian modes of worship in the forms of fir alluding to their god "Baal Berith" and palm trees for "Baal -Tammar," respectively (97). Nowadays, there is no rule stipulating that people must set up Christmas trees in their homes or die. However, it is so anchored into Christmas's ritual, and the peer pressure is so intense that if you reject Christmas trees and decorations, you will appear weird, crazy; people will think you are a fool for not aligning with the world you live in. At Christmastime, questions like "Have you set up your tree yet?" and "Are you ready for Christmas?" are the starting points of most conversations, usually accompanied by beautiful smiles. Dare to utter the words "I don't celebrate Christmas," and the smiles will quickly fade.

You can truly perceive the spirit of Nimrod hovering in people's minds—the spirit of freedom, fun, and pleasure—in the way people are invested in end-of-year celebrations. After all, these end-of-year parties are all about him, merely masquerading as pretentious Christian religious feasts, which have no biblical basis. As long as people have fun, they don't raise any question.

The myth about the tree was borrowed from a tale suggesting that "the mother of Adonis, the sun-god and great mediatorial divinity, was mystically changed into a tree, and in that state...brought forth her divine son." Her son was therefore seen as a branch, which is caricatured in Yule-log festivities on Christmas Eve. Likewise, in Chaldean mythology, it is fabled that Zero-ashta (a name meaning "seed of woman") had to enter the fire on "mother night," so that he might be "born of fire" the next day as the "branch of god," or the tree that brings all divine gifts to men (Hislop, 97).

The story of Nimrod has evolved with time. However, he has remained the center of human worship throughout ages. His devoted adepts, with the help of the devil, have rendered immortal the teachings and worship of Nimrod, which has transcended cultural boundaries since its beginning. However, they are ignorant of the truth that at the end of time, Jesus—the true Messiah—will end all sorts of lingering apostasies, and every individual who has ever lived will bow before him:

> "Therefore God exalted him to the highest place and gave him the name that is above every name, that at the name of Jesus every knee should bow, in heaven and on earth and under the earth, and every tongue acknowledge that Jesus Christ is Lord, to the glory of God the Father." (Phil. 2:9–11)

It would be quite responsible for someone to make up their mind today, bow before Jesus, and be rewarded with eternal salvation, rather than wait until they are forced to bow before him at the judgment day and then be cast into hell. Nimrod himself was a mere human being, and like everyone else, he will bow down to Jesus. Don't his followers know that judgment awaits them?

But they are experts in lies and manipulations. Through the falsification of history, the caste of Nimrod is still invested in portraying him as the divine child in its attempts to usurp the throne of Jesus. Hislop describes how they wove history into myth. In a reflection of his gruesome death, Nimrod "was symbolized as a huge tree, stripped of its branches, and cut down almost to the ground, with the great serpent, the symbol of life-restoring, twisting itself around the dead stock. And lo, at its side up sprouts a young tree of an entirely different kind, that is destined never to be cut down by hostile power." The young tree "symbolized the newborn god as Baal-Berith" ("Lord of the covenant") and depicted his everlasting power, for after being killed by his enemies, he has risen in victory over them. History recalled that in Rome, the twenty-fifth of December was celebrated as the "birthday of the unconquered sun," the day on which the vanquishing champion god resurfaced on earth. In short, the Yule log represents the corpse of Nimrod, who—though murdered and cut down by his adversaries—was deified as the resurrected sun god (Hislop, 98).

The Egyptian goddess Isis (or queen of heaven, who equated with Semiramis) had a son whose birthday, Hislop tells us, was celebrated in December, "about the time of winter solstice or Yule Day"; in fact, *Yule* in Chaldean means "Little Child" (93). Furthermore, Hislop recalls that prior to the era of Christianity, "Yule day" was celebrated on December 25 by primitive Anglo-Saxons, and the eve of twenty-fourth was called "mother night" (94). The same winter solstice was celebrated in Rome under the "feast of Saturn," a five-day celebration during which participants indulged in drinking and revelry. Slaves were granted a short period of freedom. This tradition was a complete reproduction of the primitive Babylonian festival of Bacchus (97).

In the Mistletoe's myth, the plant caricatures "the divine branch that came from heaven and grew up on a tree that sprung out of the earth," symbolizing the messiah in the same manner as the Yule log (Hislop, 98). In using a log or a tree to represent a divine branch, this myth was trying to bring heaven and earth close to each other. Given man's sinful nature, the mistletoe bough was and is still used as a symbol of reconciliation between heaven and men, which was stamped by kissing underneath it (99). Andrew stressed in his article "Why Do We Kiss Under the Mistletoe? (2013) that on Christmas Eve, wherever it was practiced, men were permitted to kiss any woman standing under the Mistletoe. Refusal of the kiss was believed to bring bad luck and was not an option for the woman.

How can pardon and reconciliation be granted by kissing someone else's wife or daughter under a tree? The Bible refers to the queen of heaven as a harlot of prostitution. The mistletoe tradition was nothing else than a path to stimulate infidelity in marriages and sex before the wedding as far as men and women were concerned—a ludicrous way to entice people to indulge in uncontrolled sex life. This way of living violates one of God's most essential and crucial laws: marriage and multiplication. People now carelessly multiply outside of marriage, leading to a widespread single-parenting mode of life and all the consequences that come with it.

In Icelandic and Scandinavian mythology, the traditional use of mistletoe sprang from Balder's tale, the Norse god and goddess Odin and Frigga's son. In the myth, Frigga learned her son was going to die, and to prevent it from happening; she made every living thing take an oath not to hurt her son. Unfortunately, she forgot to bind mistletoe to the oath, and that tree was used to murder her son (Hislop, 58). Another version gives the name Balder to a son who was resurrected; full of joy, his mother, designated mistletoe as an emblem of love and pledged to give a kiss to anyone who journeyed or toured under the tree. This practice was largely grafted into Christmas festivities in the eighteenth century (Andrews).

The dishes served at Christmas and Christmas Eve were also borrowed from Babylonian tradition. Under different names, the same god was worshipped all over the world, characterized by the same attributes and similar practices and modes of worship. In some mythologies, people believed that the boar was the animal that had murdered their god, as stipulated in the myth of Adonis, Tammuz, Cybele, and Diana. Consequently, many cultures offered the poor animal as a sacrifice to appease their god. Geese were sacrificed to the Babylonian messiah during the winter solstice, and Rome and Egypt had similar practices (102). Geese also appeared to be symbols for Seb's worship in Egypt, Cupid in Asia Minor, Brahma in India, and Juno in Rome (101).

Boar, goose, and yule cake were often cooked for these cultures' festivities, and all of these were of great significance in the worship of the primitive Babylonian messiah (Hislop,

99–101). Similar dishes have been prepared at Christmas dinners for centuries.

Halloween

Halloween is one of the most accepted end-of-year celebrations among Christians, but it is a feast also celebrated by pagans worldwide. I am stunned by this. Celebrators commonly say it is a time for fun. I always ask myself, what is fun about Halloween? What is fun about death? Death is seen in the Bible as a curse, and it came upon human because of sin. People celebrate death, yet when a loved one passes away, they lament!

It is a time of the year when I long dearly to hide until it passes away, but it is tough to do so. You must go to work or go shopping, and these excursions force you to see the monstrous decorations in people's front yards and in stores.

In his book entitled *"The Trouble with Christmas Present and Yet to Come"* (1993), Tom Flynn describes the origin of Halloween. I should first-hand make it clear that I do not endorse Flynn's atheism. Yet, in his findings, he has highlighted some truths about the end-of-year festivities that have been endorsed by so many. I chose to cite him because his findings are published in a book, compared to others whose works are laid out online without providing the name of the person who wrote the article. Nevertheless, Flynn has failed to understand the Creator of the world.

How do I know that the Bible is true? Many years ago, what has been predicted in the Old Testament has come to pass, with all its details and precision, exactly as expected. Countering all the myths and confusion laid out by Semiramis and Nimrod, the true God wanted to reveal himself to humankind, and it was not an easy task, given the wrong beliefs and worship humanity had already been indulging themselves in for ages.

The prime example of the truth of the Bible is Isaiah's prediction of the birth of Jesus Christ—about seven hundred years before it came to pass: "Therefore, the Lord Himself will give you a sign: Behold, the virgin shall conceive and bear a Son, and shall call His name Immanuel" (Isa. 7:14). The same prophecy was quoted in the gospels (Matt. 1:23) to remind the Jews at that time that the birth of Jesus Christ was not a random event; instead, God had planned it ahead of time, and two thousand years ago, he executed that plan to draw humanity back to the true Messiah, authentic worship, and true salvation (which can only happen through the real Savior and not the usurper, Nimrod).

In addition, when the magi arrived in Jerusalem by following the stars, they inadvertently alerted Herod to the event when they asked him where the Baby God was residing. Herod then summoned the chief priests and asked them where the Messiah was to be born (Matt. 2:3). The chief priests responded by quoting the passage in the Old Testament that accurately predicted the coming of the Messiah:

> But you, Bethlehem Ephrathah,
> > though you are small among the clans of Judah,
> out of you will come for me
> > one who will be ruler over Israel,
> whose origins are from of old,
> > from ancient
> > times." (Mic. 5:2)

Let's go back to the origin of Halloween. Flynn mentions that the Norse god Odin was also known by the names Jólnir and Woden. In Norse mythology, Odin was the husband of the goddess Frigga (also called Frigg or Bestla; Wikipedia 2020), the queen of heaven. Myths portrayed Odin as a cosmic outlaw riding on a white horse (Flynn 1993, 46), accompanied by demons. Norse religion adherents also believed that evil spirits resided in the woods and mountains and that those spirits were restless, especially during Yule at the harvest festival. With time came the habit of setting out food offerings to appease those night-time spirits (46). Also rooted in their culture was the notion of a goddess who would pay a visit to every home on the New Year's Eve, and people were invited to provide food for her. Down the road, these traditions would relate to Halloween, which was birthed from the All Hallows' Day (47).

In her article "The History of Trick or Treating Is Weirder Than You Thought" (2012), Eveleth stressed that the Celts also believed of evil spirits roaming free at the end of the year. To protect themselves, the Celts would wear scary garments, aiming at confusing the demons so that the monsters would not notice the presence of human beings while they are journeying on earth, but thinking that they are one of them. It was some camouflage, like what the chameleons do. November 1 of each year was the day when the Celts not only celebrated their New Year but also was the day when the wearing of scary garments took place. Kids dress up in those scary costumes would "go around door to door begging for food and money in exchange for songs and prayers, often said on behalf of the dead" (Eveleth, 2012).

In quest of members, the Catholic Church embraced pagan celebrations again, turning the pagan demon-like exhibition into a religious festivity and calling it "All Saints' Day" or "Hallows' Day" (Eveleth). The Catholic Church kept the same November 1 to commemorate the so-called "saints" who had died and gone to heaven. The canonization of saints is one of the great apostasies of the Catholic Church; humans dared to carry out the role of judge—a role that the Creator of the universe assigned only to his Son Jesus.

When Samuel was selecting the first king of Israel, God said to him, "Do not consider his appearance or his height, for I have rejected him. The LORD does not look at the things people look at. People look at the outward appearance, but the LORD looks at the heart" (1 Sam. 16:7). God alone is capable of judging justly; thus, the throne of judgment is granted to Jesus alone:

> "But when the Son of Man comes in His glory, and all the angels with Him, then He will sit on

His glorious throne. And all the nations will be gathered before Him; and He will separate them from one another, as the shepherd separates the sheep from the goats." (Matt. 25:31–32)

With the change of calendar (which would now begin in January) brought about by the Roman Catholic Church, the coming of "Berchta" was moved to December 6. Down the road, it would be celebrated as the feast of St. Nicholas (Flynn, 48) to masquerade the true meaning of such a celebration. I firmly believe that the change in the calendar was not merely an innocent move. The purpose was to bring order to all the mess and confusion that lingered in the church, leading people—and especially Catholic votaries—into unknowingly remaining faithful to the worship of Nimrod and Semiramis. Flynn recalled that in Europe during the holidays, boys wore scary costumes with a headpiece resembling a horse's head. One of the Names given to the horse was "old Hob," and some would light candles in its eyes and go from home to home begging for gifts. He notes that "the carved face lighted by a flickering candle is an effect American families recapture when they carve their Halloween jack-o-lanterns" (49). The concept of trick-or-treating can also be traced back to Scotland, where poor kids on New Year's Eve would go house to house begging for oatcake; this lasted until about the middle of the nineteenth century (49).

Hislop stated that because of the kind of death Nimrod went through, being murdered and decapitated, his worshippers commemorated his fate through slashing and cutting their bodies. This practice is seen in the worship of Osiris, Bellona, Saturn, Moloch, Tammuz, and Baal (151–53). These gods were believed by their worshippers to have undergone the ordeal of decapitation, and "they looked upon the shedding of their blood as a most meritorious of penance" (153), which has been endorsed by the Roman Catholic Church. For example, the early Catholic pilgrims in Ireland were seen walking on their knees over sharp stones; another group, the flagellants, flogged themselves in public. Moreover, on Good Fridays, some would lash themselves until blood was shed to commemorate the suffering of Jesus Christ, precisely like Osiris's worshippers did (154). This mode of worship was also seen among the Israelites who rejected their God for pagan worship long before the birth of Jesus Christ and the Almighty condemned it:

> "They do not cry out to me from their hearts
>   but wail on their beds.
> They slash themselves, appealing to their gods
>   for grain and new wine, but
>   they turn away from me".
> (Hosea 7:14)

All these evil practices—borrowed from the mysteries of Babylon—are now recaptured at Halloween in costume designs, fashions, and gadgets.

CHAPTER 6

Other Religious Festivities Borrowed from Babylonians

Easter

WHEN I WAS SEARCHING OUT data for this book, I stumbled across the blog of J'aime Rubio—what a fascinating blog! After I read her thoughts on Christmas and Halloween, I was about to leave the page when her rubric of Easter caught my eye. *What does she have to say about Easter?* I asked myself. After all, it was not a controversial celebration like the two others.

After a little bit of reluctance, I decided to go ahead and read it. By the time I left the page, I could not believe what I had just read. Easter—the name used to commemorate the death and resurrection of my Lord Jesus Christ—is of pagan origin as well. Stunning, bewildering, and unbelievable! How had I never heard about this in any discussion, neither in the church nor anywhere else? Was it true?

I searched the *Merriam-Webster Dictionary*, which defined *Easter* as "a feast that commemorates Christ's resurrection and is observed with variations of date due to different calendars on the first Sunday after the paschal full moon." This is the definition common people like me know.

But let's see what Hislop has to say about it. He stresses that Easter is of Chaldean origin and refers to Astarte, which is another title of Beltis, the queen of heaven, known as Ishtar to primitive Assyrians, which links these goddesses to Semiramis. In April each year, the Assyrians organized a solemn religious feast for their god, and it was called Easter-Monath. The Passover of Jesus, as celebrated by the early Christian church, was never known by the name of Easter; instead, it was the Roman Catholic Church that, in the second century, chose to undermine the Passover of Christ by giving it a pagan name, thereby masquerading the worship of Semiramis under the guise of Christianity (Hislop, 103).

The first Christians celebrated Passover (not Easter) alongside the Jewish festival on the night of Nisan 15, which is the first day of the festival of Unleavened Bread on which the passover lamb had to be sacrificed. However, Passover has different meanings for each congregation. While the Jews celebrate it to commemorate their forefathers' liberation from slavery in Egypt, early Christians commemorate the betrayal and crucifixion of Jesus on that same day. It is that crucifixion that paved the way to salvation of humankind. It is commonly said that Sunday was chosen as the day of worship because Jesus resurrected on a Sunday. Right! Does a human have the power to bring a chance to the will of the Almighty? In the old testament, not keeping the Sabbath holy was an offense punishable by death sentence (Exodus 31:15).—yet another scheme put forth by the devil to sabotage the Lord's Sabbath.

Not only that, but the birthday of Jesus Christ, which is nowhere found in the Bible, has also been imposed by Rome and is now widely accepted and celebrated. Rome now dictates the mode of wor-ship, not the Bible, not Jesus. Jesus stressed that his church is built on the foundation of apostles and prophets, with him as the chief cornerstone (Eph. 2:20). Yet people accept the one built by the pope and his bishops, for it is during their synodical meetings that all those new doctrines and changes came about (Church of God International). Some Christian denominations nowadays endorse and passively celebrate these changes as if they were quite normal and evident. True Christians all over the world should consider going back to worshipping our Savior on the Sabbath.

Not only is Easter of pagan origin, but the fasting around Passover (recommended by the Roman Catholic since about the year 519 and observed by most Christian denominations around the world) is of pagan origin as well. Hislop has traced the origin of spring fasting to Tammuz's early worship, in which fasting was accompanied by weeping and wailing to commemorate the death and resurrection of Tammuz, who was murdered. Similarly, Mexicans observe forty days of fasting; Egyptians observed forty days of fasting to commemorate the sun god, Osiris; and Greeks did the same for the gods Proserpine and Bacchus (Hislop 105, 107).

Easter, as celebrated today is no different from what was done before Christianity. The dyed eggs and hot cross buns of Good Friday can be traced back to the primitive Babylonian mode of worshipping the queen of heaven, when they gave buns in offering and consecrated eggs (Hislop, 108). Even the Israelites offered bread in worship to the queen of heaven, which roused the Lord's anger:

> "The children gather wood, the fathers light the fire, and the women knead the dough and make cakes to offer to the Queen of Heaven. They pour out drink offerings to other gods to arouse my anger. But am I the one they are provoking? declares the Lord. Are they not rather harming themselves, to their own shame?
>
> "Therefore, this is what the Sovereign Lord says: My anger and my wrath will be poured out on this place—on man and beast, on the trees of the field and on the crops of your land—and it will burn and not be quenched." (Jer. 7:18–20)

Hindus similarly celebrated the golden egg, which they believe to be the source of life and the whole creation (Jayaram 2019). The people of China also use dyed eggs in their worship till today, and the people of Athens consecrated an egg to Bacchus (Hislop, 108), which symbolized rebirth. The use of egg in religious practices is also traced back to ancient Egyptians, who believed that Venus had come from an egg that had fallen from heaven; Venus was also worshipped in Syria and Cyprus under the names Astarte and Easter (109). In every country where eggs were used in worship, they basically carried the same meaning, hearkening back to the ark in which Noah and his family were locked up till the water subsided, like a "chick is enclosed in the egg before hatching." The ark, as the "egg in which the world was shut up," was "granted… the name of the 'mundane egg'" (109).

Hislop stresses that in Hebrew, *egg* is spelled *Baitz* (or *Baith* in Chaldean and Phoenician), meaning "house." So "the egg floating on the waters that contained the world was the house floating on the water of the deluge, with the element of the new world in its bosom" (110). The fable of the egg coming from heaven likely refers to the preparation and construction of the ark under the request of God, who dwells in heaven. As depicted in Chaldean fables, Astarte was kept in the ark during the flood and was given the attributes of an emancipator, of one by whom human beings are ever blessed, and of "the great civilizer" (110)—the same attributes given to Nimrod and his mother by their early worshippers.

The truth is that both were born after the flood. According to the biblical genealogy, Nimrod is the grandson of Noah, who built the ark, but there is no mentioned of any of Noah's grandsons being in the ark: "Noah was six hundred years old when the floodwaters came on the earth. And Noah and his sons and his wife and his sons' wives entered the ark to escape the waters of the flood" (Gen. 7:6–7). However, the primitive Babylonian worshippers seemed to believe that the queen of heaven had lived before the flood and had passed through it safely (Hislop, 110).

According to Hislop, the early Roman church adopted this mystic egg of Astarte and consecrated it as a symbol of Christ's resurrection," and Pope Paul V even mentioned it in one of the prayers he taught at Easter, saying, "Bless, O Lord, we beseech thee, this thy creature of egg, that it may become a wholesome sustenance unto thy servants, eating it in remembrance of our Lord Jesus Christ" (Hislop, 110).

The Babylonians also used the pomegranate as a symbol of Easter. One of the ancient sculptures of the queen of heaven, also called "*Idaia Mater, Astarte, Cybele*," showed her holding a pomegranate. According to Chaldean mythology, the queen of heaven was worshipped on a secret mountain called *Mount Idaia or Ida,* which means the "Mountain of Knowledge" (Hislop, 111). *Idaia Mater* meant the "mother of knowledge" or the "Mother Eve" (110). Eve in the Bible is the one who committed the first sin by coveting the knowledge of good and evil, a sin that carried a dreadful price for her and her offspring. So, representing Astarte holding a fruit was a sort of invitation to her worshippers to partake in her mysteries, which suggests that the pomegranate could have been the fruit of the forbidden tree of the knowledge of good and evil (111).

The Bible presented the act of eating the forbidden fruit as the fall of humanity. However, the devil turns it upside down and presents it as a victory, as the way by which humans gained knowledge and blessings that otherwise would have been inaccessible. He portrays these as having come from great benefactors—that is, from Nimrod and Semiramis—from who comes perfection and every good thing (Hislop, 111). This upside-down story is caricatured in Greek mythology, which presents Hercules as the great deliverer, the one who set humans free from God's yoke by allowing them to eat the forbidden fruit, without which knowledge and wisdom remains concealed. It also presents Jehovah as the serpent, the mean and unloved one who, wanting men to stay unwise, forbade them to eat the very fruit that would grant them wisdom (113). What a grand, evil scheme the devil has created: a saddening call for rebellion against the true God and Creator of the universe, a path to perdition for many souls.

The Sign of the Cross

While I was writing this book, I decided to address the cross as the Catholic Church portrays it. Given that Jesus was crucified on a cross, I had never questioned its use as a symbol of faith, so prevalently used that no prayer, no mass, and no religious practice can occur in the Catholic Church without it.

Earlier, I had also heard of the upside-down cross, which is said to be the devil's symbol. Furthermore, Rome has come up with the story that the Apostle Paul asked to be crucified upside-down because he considered himself unworthy to die the same death as did his Lord and Savior Jesus Christ. It is a very appealing tale, but is it a fairy tale or the truth? After all the aforementioned findings, any customs or practices carried on in the Catholic Church are now questionable to me. Since I left the Catholic Church, I have quit making the sign of cross before and after prayer. Therefore, when it came to my mind, I studied it and made a drawing of what that symbol really looks like when your right hand goes from your forehead down to your chest and across from one shoulder to the other. The conclusion was stunning and unbelievable. The sign Catholic votaries make is *not* a cross—it is an upside-down cross!

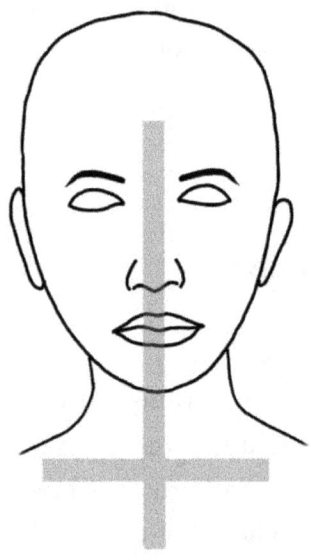

On the one hand, if we assume that Paul's story is true, the use of this sign raises Paul's work above that of Christ, if they are knowingly using the symbol of the upside-down cross as an emblem of faith. On the other hand, it could be the symbol of Satan, which Rome has knowingly raised as the banner for their religious faith: After all, they know that it is not Jesus they are bringing to their votaries in worship but Nimrod. I truly feel sorry for those who blindly put their trust in Rome and the Pope. Look at the Catholic votaries' excitement in the street when their so call infallible Pope visits them. Sad! Lord, have mercy!

While reading Hislop's book, I was happy and grateful to see that he, too, addresses the cross's topic. Before Christ, the cross existed solely as a means of execution. What a dreadful and excruciating way to die! I used to ask myself how people ever thought of such a severe form of punishment. The above findings are a clear answer to that question. If Nimrod's worshippers did not even look upon themselves with mercy, why would they care or feel for someone dying on the cross? They cut and slashed themselves and even burned their kids alive as sacrifices to Tammuz. Hislop stresses that the cross originated from the Babylonian mysteries. It is as simple as you might think: "the letter T is the initial of the name Tammuz" (Hislop, 197). Now, how is the Roman cross similar to the Tammuz cross? Hislop states that Rome views the cross as "the tree of life," and worshippers are called to address it by saying,

> "Hail, O Cross, triumphal wood, true salvation of the world, among trees there is none like thee in leaf, flower, and bud. O cross, our only hope, increase righteousness to the godly and pardon the offenses of the guilty." (200)

"Idol Worship in Christianity" covers some pagan dogmas or myths replicated in the Roman Catholic Church, but this list is not exhaustive. Nearly every single element, design, practice, or mode of worship displayed in that Church is a mere duplication of the Babylonian pagan worship method. I strongly recommend *The Two Babylons*, Hislop's book, to my readers. Among other topics, it explains how calling Mary the mediator between Jesus and men reflects the role of Semiramis (Hislop, 157);

How the purification of water with salt is pure demon worship (138);

How the Catholic Church's doctrines of judgment; justification by deeds is unbiblical (146–47);

The purgatory; and prayers for the dead (167) keep Catholic votaries from any thought of repentance or growth in faith. After all, their name tag as Catholic supposedly grants them salvation, so even if death suddenly cuts them off, their souls will sojourn in purgatory until they are purified. Therefore, everyone will be safe. What a lie! That is not in the Bible at all.

How popes are not the only people that were ever called "sovereign pontiff" but has borrowed it or copied "the model of original grand Council of Pontiffs at Babylon" (206). Likewise, the college of nuns and that of monks are mere duplications of the Babylonian hierarchical order of their institutions' body. In this closed society, ladies were called to single life and maintain their purity throughout their life of services (223).

How Peter's key is unbiblical and is, without the shadow of a doubt, the key used as the symbol of god Cybele and Janus's power before Christianity: gods worshipped in ancient Rome(206-207).

CHAPTER 7

Passages Found in the Bible That Condemn Carved Objects Called Gods

VIII. The book of Exodus

Exodus 20: 4-6 "You shall not make for yourself an image in the form of anything in heaven above or on the earth beneath or in the waters below. You shall not bow down to them or worship them; for I, the LORD your God, am a jealous God, punishing the children for the sin of the parents to the third and fourth generation of those who hate me, but showing love to a thousand generations of those who love me and keep my commandments".

Exodus 20: 22-23 "Then the LORD said to Moses, "Tell the Israelites this: 'You have seen for yourselves that I have spoken to you from heaven: Do not make any gods to be alongside me; do not make for yourselves gods of silver or gods of gold".

Exodus 23: 32-33 "Do not make a covenant with them or with their gods. Do not let them live in your land or they will cause you to sin against me, because the worship of their gods will certainly be a snare to you."

Exodus 32: 4 "He took what they handed him and made it into an idol cast in the shape of a calf, fashioning it with a tool. Then they said, "These are your gods, Israel, who brought you up out of Egypt." Isn't this a great lie? Where was that idol when the Almighty was using plagues to shake up pharaoh in order to get them out of Egypt; when the almighty parted the red sea and walked them through. They just finish fashion that useless object and attributed to it, a work that was carried out a couple of days, month ago"

Exodus 32: 31 "So Moses went back to the Lord and said, "Oh, what a great sin these people have committed! They have made themselves gods of gold. But now, please forgive their sin—but if not, then blot me out of the book you have written."

Exodus 32: 35 "And the Lord struck the people with a plague because of what they did with the calf Aaron had made".

Exodus 34: 12-17 "Obey what I command you today. I will drive out before you the Amorites, Canaanites, Hittites, Perizzites, Hivites and Jebusites. Be careful not to make a treaty with those who live in the land where you are going, or they will be a snare among you. Break down their altars, smash their sacred stones and cut down their Asherah poles. Do not worship any other god, for the Lord, whose name is Jealous, is a jealous God". "Be careful not to make a treaty with those who live in the land; for when they prostitute themselves to their gods and sacrifice to them, they will invite you and you will eat their sacrifices. And when you choose some of their daughters as wives for your sons and those daughters prostitute themselves to their gods, they will lead your sons to do the same. "Do not make any idols".

IX. The Book of Leviticus

Leviticus 17: 7 "They must no longer offer any of their sacrifices to the goat idols to whom they prostitute themselves. This is to be a lasting ordinance for them and for the generations to come".

Leviticus 19:4 "Do not turn to idols or make metal gods for yourselves. I am the Lord your God".

Leviticus 26:1 "Do not make idols or set up an image or a sacred stone for yourselves, and do not place a carved stone in your land to bow down before it. I am the Lord your God".

Leviticus 26: 30 "I will destroy your high places, cut down your incense altars and pile your dead bodies on the lifeless forms of your idols, and I will abhor you".

X. The Book of Numbers

Numbers 25:1-3 "While Israel was staying in Shittim, the men began to indulge in sexual immorality with Moabite women, who invited them to the sacrifices to their gods. The people ate the sacrificial meal and bowed down before these gods. So Israel yoked themselves to the Baal of Peor. And the LORD's anger burned against them".

Numbers 25: 5 "So Moses said to Israel's judges, "Each of you must put to death those of your people who have yoked themselves to the Baal of Peor."

Numbers 33:3- 4 "The Israelites set out from Rameses on the fifteenth day of the first month, the day after the Passover. They marched out defiantly in full view of all the Egyptians, who were burying all their firstborn, whom the LORD had struck down among them; for the LORD had brought judgment on their gods".

Numbers 33:52 "drive out all the inhabitants of the land before you. Destroy all their carved images and their cast idols and demolish all their high places".

XI. The Book of Deuteronomy

Deuteronomy 4:2-3 "Do not add to what I command you and do not subtract from it, but keep the commands of the Lord your God that I give you. You saw with your own eyes what the Lord did at Baal Peor. The Lord your God destroyed from among you everyone who followed the Baal of Peor, but all of you who held fast to the Lord your God are still alive today".

Deuteronomy 4:7-19 "What other nation is so great as to have their gods near them the way the Lord our God is near us whenever we pray to him? And what other nation is so great as to have such righteous decrees and laws as this body of laws I am setting before you today? Only be careful and watch yourselves closely so that you do not forget the things your eyes have seen or let them fade from your heart as long as you live. Teach them to your children and to their children after them. Remember the day you stood before the Lord your God at Horeb, when he said to me, "Assemble the people before me to hear my words so that they may learn to revere me as long as they live in the land and may teach them to their children". You came near and stood at the foot of the mountain while it blazed with fire to the very heavens, with black clouds and deep darkness. Then the Lord spoke to you out of the fire. You heard the sound of words but saw no form; there was only a voice... You saw no form of any kind the day the Lord spoke to you at Horeb out of the fire. Therefore watch yourselves very carefully, so that you do not become corrupt and make for yourselves an idol, an image of any shape, whether formed like a man or a woman, or like any animal on earth or any bird that flies in the air, or like any creature that moves along the ground or any fish in the waters below. And when you look up to the sky and see the sun, the moon and the stars—all the heavenly array—do not be enticed into bowing down to them and worshiping things the Lord your God has apportioned to all the nations under heaven".

Deuteronomy 4: 23-28 "Be careful not to forget the covenant of the Lord your God that he made with you; do not make for yourselves an idol in the form of anything the Lord your God has forbidden. For the Lord your God is a consuming fire, a jealous God. After you have had children and grandchildren and have lived in the land a long time—if you then become corrupt and make any kind of idol, doing evil in the eyes of the Lord your God and arousing his anger, I call the heavens and the earth as witnesses against you this day that you will quickly perish from the land that you are crossing the Jordan to possess. The Lord will scatter you among the peoples, and only a few of you will survive among the nations to which the Lord will drive you. There you will worship man-made gods of wood and stone, which cannot see or hear or eat or smell".

Deuteronomy 5: 8-10 "You shall not make for yourself an image in the form of anything in heaven above or on the earth beneath or in the waters below. You shall not bow down to them or worship them; for I, the Lord your God, am a jealous God, punishing the children for the sin of the parents to the third and fourth generation of those who hate me, but showing love to a thousand generations of those who love me and keep my commandments".

Deuteronomy 6:14-15 "Do not follow other gods, the gods of the peoples around you; for the LORD your God, who is among you, is a jealous God and his anger will burn against you, and he will destroy you from the face of the land".

Deuteronomy 7:3-6 "Do not intermarry with them. Do not give your daughters to their sons or take their daughters for your sons, for they will turn your children away from following me to serve other gods, and the LORD's anger will burn against you and will quickly destroy you. This is what you are to do to them: Break down their altars, smash their sacred stones, cut down their Asherah poles and burn their idols in the fire. For you are a people holy to the LORD your God. The LORD your God has chosen you out of all the peoples on the face of the earth to be his people, his treasured possession".

Deuteronomy 7:16 "You must destroy all the peoples the LORD your God gives over to you. Do not look on them with pity and do not serve their gods, for that will be a snare to you".

Deuteronomy 7:25-26 "The images of their gods you are to burn in the fire. Do not covet the silver and gold on them, and do not take it for yourselves, or you will be ensnared by it, for it is detestable to the LORD your God. Do not bring a detestable thing into your house or you, like it, will be set apart for destruction. Regard it as vile and utterly detest it, for it is set apart for destruction".

Deuteronomy 8:19-20 "If you ever forget the Lord your God and follow other gods and worship and bow down to them, I testify against you today that you will surely be destroyed. Like the nations the Lord destroyed before you, so you will be destroyed for not obeying the Lord your God".

Deuteronomy 9:12 "Then the Lord told me, "Go down from here at once, because your people whom you brought out of Egypt have become corrupt. They have turned away quickly from what I commanded them and have made an idol for themselves."

Deuteronomy 9:16-17 "When I looked, I saw that you had sinned against the Lord your God; you had made for yourselves an idol cast in the shape of a calf. You had turned aside quickly from the way that the Lord had commanded you. So, I took the two tablets and threw them out of my hands, breaking them to pieces before your eyes".

Deuteronomy 9:21 "Also I took that sinful thing of yours, the calf you had made, and burned it in the fire. Then I crushed it and ground it to powder as fine as dust and threw the dust into a stream that flowed down the mountain".

Deuteronomy 12:2-4 "Destroy completely all the places on the high mountains, on the hills and under every spreading tree, where the nations you are dispossessing worship their gods. Break down their altars, smash their sacred stones and burn their Asherah poles in the fire; cut down the idols of their gods and wipe out their names from those places. You must not worship the Lord your God in their way."

Deuteronomy 12: 29-31 "...But when you have driven them out and settled in their land, and after they have been destroyed before you, be careful not to be ensnared by inquiring about their gods, saying, "How do these nations serve their gods? We will do the same." You must not worship the Lord your God in their way, because in worshiping their gods, they do all kinds of detestable things the Lord hates. They even burn their sons and daughters in the fire as sacrifices to their gods".

Deuteronomy 13:1-3 "If a prophet, or one who foretells by dreams, appears among you and announces to you a sign or wonder, and if the sign or wonder spoken of takes place, and the prophet says, "Let us follow other gods" (gods you have not known) "and let us worship them," you must not listen to the words of that prophet or dreamer".

Deuteronomy 13:6-15 "If your very own brother, or your son or daughter, or the wife you love, or your closest friend secretly entices you, saying, "Let us go and worship other gods" (gods that neither you nor your ancestors have known, gods of the peoples around you, whether near or far, from one end of the land to the other), do not yield to them or listen to them. Show them no pity. Do not spare them or shield them. You must certainly put them to death. Your hand must be the first in putting them to death, and then the hands of all the people. Stone them to death, because they tried to turn you away from the LORD your God, who brought you out of Egypt, out of the land of slavery. Then all Israel will hear and be afraid, and no one among you will do such an evil thing again. If you hear it said about one of the towns the LORD your God is giving you to live in that troublemakers have arisen among you and have led the people of their town astray, saying, "Let us go and worship other gods" (gods you have not known), then you must inquire, probe and investigate it thoroughly. And if it is true and it has been proved that this detestable thing has been done among you, you must certainly put to the sword all who live in that town. You must destroy it completely, both its people and its livestock".

Deuteronomy 16: 21-22 "Do not set up any wooden Asherah pole beside the altar you build to the LORD your God, and do not erect a sacred stone, for these the LORD your God hates".

Deuteronomy 17: 2-6 "If a man or woman living among you in one of the towns the LORD gives you is found doing evil in the eyes of the LORD your God in violation of his covenant, and contrary to my command has worshiped other gods, bowing down to them or to the sun or the moon or the stars in the sky, and this has been brought to your attention, then you must investigate it thoroughly. If it is true and it has been proved that this detestable thing has been done in Israel, take the man or woman who has done this evil deed to your city gate and stone that person to death. On the testimony of two or three witnesses a person is to be put to death".

Deuteronomy 27:15 "Cursed is anyone who makes an idol—a thing detestable to the Lord, the work of skilled hands—and sets it up in secret."

Deuteronomy 28:36-37, 64 "The Lord will drive you and the king you set over you to a nation unknown to you or your ancestors. There you will worship other gods, gods of wood and stone. You will become a thing of horror, a byword and an object of ridicule among all the peoples where the Lord will drive you.... Then the Lord will scatter you among all nations, from one end of the earth to the other. There you will worship other gods—gods of wood and stone, which neither you nor your ancestors have known".

Deuteronomy 29:17-18 "You saw among them their detestable images and idols of wood and stone, of silver and gold. Make sure there is no man or woman, clan or tribe among you today whose heart turns away from the Lord our God to go and worship the gods of those nations; make sure there is no root among you that produces such bitter poison".

Deuteronomy 29: 26 "They went off and worshiped other gods and bowed down to them, gods they did not know, gods he had not given them".

Deuteronomy 30: 17-18 "But if your heart turns away and you are not obedient, and if you are drawn away to bow down to other gods and worship them, I declare to you this day that you will certainly be destroyed. You will not live long in the land you are crossing the Jordan to enter and possess".

Deuteronomy 31: 16 & 18, 20 "And the LORD said to Moses: "You are going to rest with your ancestors, and these people will soon prostitute themselves to the foreign gods of the land they are entering. They will forsake me and break the covenant I made with them… And I will certainly hide my face in that day because of all their wickedness in turning to other gods… When I have brought them into the land flowing with milk and honey, the land I promised on oath to their ancestors, and when they eat their fill and thrive, they will turn to other gods and worship them, rejecting me and breaking my covenant".

Deuteronomy 32: 16-17, 21, 37-39 "They made him jealous with their foreign gods and angered him with their detestable idols. They sacrificed to false gods, which are not God— gods they had not known, gods that recently appeared, gods your ancestors did not fear…They made me jealous by what is no god and angered me with their worthless idols. I will make them envious by those who are not a people; I will make them angry by a nation that has no understanding… He will say: "Now where are their gods, the rock they took refuge in, the gods who ate the fat of their sacrifices and drank the wine of their drink offerings? Let them rise up to help you! Let them give you shelter! "See now that I myself am he! There is no god besides me".

XII. The book of Joshua

Joshua 23: 7, 16 "Do not associate with these nations that remain among you; do not invoke the names of their gods or swear by them. You must not serve them or bow down to them. ⁸ But you are to hold fast to the LORD your God, as you have until now. If you violate the covenant of the LORD your God, which he commanded you, and go and serve other gods and bow down to them, the LORD's anger will burn against you, and you will quickly perish from the good land he has given you."

Joshua 24: 2, 14-16 "Joshua said to all the people, "This is what the LORD, the God of Israel, says: 'Long ago your ancestors, including Terah the father of Abraham and Nahor, lived beyond the Euphrates River and worshiped other gods. "Now fear the LORD and serve him with all faithfulness. Throw away the gods your ancestors worshiped beyond the Euphrates River and in Egypt and serve the LORD. But if serving the LORD seems undesirable to you, then choose for yourselves this day whom you will serve, whether the gods your ancestors served beyond the Euphrates, or the gods of the Amorites, in whose land you are living. But as for me and my household, we will serve the LORD." Then the people answered, "Far be it from us to forsake the LORD to serve other gods!"

Joshua 24: 20-24 "If you forsake the LORD and serve foreign gods, he will turn and bring disaster on you and make an end of you, after he has been good to you." But the people said to Joshua, "No! We will serve the LORD." "Then Joshua said, "You are witnesses against yourselves that you have chosen to serve the LORD." "Yes, we are witnesses," they replied. "Now then," said Joshua, "throw away the foreign gods that are among you and yield your hearts to the LORD, the God of Israel." And the people said to Joshua, "We will serve the LORD our God and obey him."

XIII. The book of Judges

Judges 2: 2, 10-13 "I said, 'I will never break my covenant with you, and you shall not make a covenant with the people of this land, but you shall break down their altars.' Yet you have disobeyed me. Why have you done this?... After that whole generation had been gathered to their ancestors, another generation grew up who knew neither the LORD nor what he had done for Israel. Then the Israelites did evil in the eyes of the LORD and served the Baals. They forsook the LORD, the God of their ancestors, who had brought them out of Egypt. They followed and worshiped various gods of the peoples around them. They aroused the LORD's anger because they forsook him and served Baal and the Ashtoreths".

Judges 2: 17-19 "Yet they would not listen to their judges but prostituted themselves to other gods and worshiped them. They quickly turned from the ways of their ancestors, who had been obedient to the LORD's commands. Whenever the LORD raised up a judge for them, he was with the judge and saved them out of the hands of their enemies as long as the judge lived; for the LORD relented because of their groaning under those who oppressed and afflicted them. But when the judge died, the people returned to ways even more corrupt than those of their ancestors, following other gods and serving and worshiping them. They refused to give up their evil practices and stubborn ways".

Judges 3: 6-7 "They took their daughters in marriage and gave their own daughters to their sons and served their gods. The Israelites did evil in the eyes of the LORD; they forgot the LORD their God and served the Baals and the Asherahs".

Judges 6:10, 25-31 "I said to you, 'I am the LORD your God; do not worship the gods of the Amorites, in whose land you live.' But you have not listened to me" ... That same night the LORD said to him, "Take the second bull from your father's herd, the one seven years old. Tear down your father's altar to Baal and cut down the Asherah pole beside it. Then build a proper kind of altar to the LORD your God on the top of this height. Using the wood of the Asherah pole that you cut down, offer the second bull as a burnt offering." So, Gideon took ten of his servants and did as the LORD told him. But because he was afraid of his family and the townspeople, he did it at night rather than in the daytime. In the morning when the people of the town got up, there was Baal's altar, demolished, with the Asherah pole beside it cut down and the second bull sacrificed on the newly built altar! They asked each other, "Who did this?" When they carefully investigated, they were told, "Gideon son of Joash did it." The people of the town demanded of Joash, "Bring out your son. He must die, because he has broken down Baal's altar and cut down the Asherah pole beside it." But Joash replied to the hostile crowd around him, "Are you going to plead Baal's cause? Are you trying to save him? Whoever fights for him shall be put to death by morning! If Baal really is a god, he can defend himself when someone breaks down his altar." So because Gideon broke down Baal's altar, they gave him the name Jerub-Baal that day, saying, "Let Baal contend with him."

Judges 8: 27, 33-34 "Gideon made the gold into an ephod, which he placed in Ophrah, his town. All Israel prostituted themselves by worshiping it there, and it became a snare to Gideon and his family... No sooner had Gideon died than the Israelites again prostituted themselves to the Baals. They set up Baal-Berith as their god and did not remember the LORD their God, who had rescued them from the hands of all their enemies on every side".

Judges 10: 6, 10-16 "Again the Israelites did evil in the eyes of the LORD. They served the Baals and the Ashtoreths, and the gods of Aram, the gods of Sidon, the gods of Moab, the gods of the Ammonites and the gods of the Philistines. And because the Israelites forsook the LORD and no longer served him… Then the Israelites cried out to the LORD, "We have sinned against you, forsaking our God and serving the Baals." The LORD replied, "When the Egyptians, the Amorites, the Ammonites, the Philistines, the Sidonians, the Amalekites and the Maonites oppressed you and you cried to me for help, did I not save you from their hands? But you have forsaken me and served other gods, so I will no longer save you. Go and cry out to the gods you have chosen. Let them save you when you are in trouble!" But the Israelites said to the LORD, "We have sinned. Do with us whatever you think best, but please rescue us now." Then they got rid of the foreign gods among them and served the LORD. And he could bear Israel's misery no longer".

Judges 17: 3-5 "When he returned the eleven hundred shekels of silver to his mother, she said, "I solemnly consecrate my silver to the LORD for my son to make an image overlaid with silver. I will give it back to you." So after he returned the silver to his mother, she took two hundred shekels of silver and gave them to a silversmith, who used them to make the idol. And it was put in Micah's house. Now this man Micah had a shrine, and he made an ephod and some household gods and installed one of his sons as his priest".

Judges 18: 14-31 "Then the five men who had spied out the land of Laish said to their fellow Danites, "Do you know that one of these houses has an ephod, some household gods and an image overlaid with silver? Now you know what to do." So, they turned in there and went to the house of the young Levite at Micah's place and greeted him. The six hundred Danites, armed for battle, stood at the entrance of the gate. The five men who had spied out the land went inside and took the idol, the ephod and the household gods while the priest and the six hundred armed men stood at the entrance of the gate. When the five men went into Micah's house and took the idol, the ephod and the household gods, the priest said to them, "What are you doing?" They answered him, "Be quiet! Don't say a word. Come with us and be our father and priest. Isn't it better that you serve a tribe and clan in Israel as priest rather than just one man's household?" The priest was very pleased. He took the ephod, the household gods and the idol and went along with the people. Putting their little children, their livestock and their possessions in front of them, they turned away and left. When they had gone some distance from Micah's house, the men who lived near Micah were called together and overtook the Danites. As they shouted after them, the Danites turned and said to Micah, "What's the matter with you that you called out your men to fight?" He replied, "You took the gods I made, and my priest, and went away. What else do I have? How can you ask, 'What's the matter with you?" The Danites answered, "Don't argue with us, or some of the men may get angry and attack you, and you and your family will lose your lives." So, the Danites went their way, and Micah, seeing that they were too strong for him, turned around and went back home. Then they took what Micah had made, and his priest, and went on to Laish, against a people at peace and secure. They attacked them with the sword and burned down their city. There was no one to rescue them because they lived a long way from Sidon and had no relationship with anyone else. The city was in a valley near Beth Rehob. The Danites rebuilt the city and settled there. They named it Dan after their ancestor Dan, who was born to Israel—though the city used to be called Laish. There the Danites set up for themselves the idol, and Jonathan son of Gershom, the son of Moses, and his sons were priests for the tribe of Dan until the time of the captivity of the land. They continued to use the idol Micah had made, all the time the house of God was in Shiloh".

XIV. The book of Ruth

Ruth 1: 15-16 "Look," said Naomi, "your sister-in-law is going back to her people and her gods. Go back with her" But Ruth replied, "Don't urge me to leave you or to turn back from you. Where you go, I will go, and where you stay, I will stay. Your people will be my people and your God my God".

XV. The Book of I Samuel

1 Samuel 5: 1-4 "After the Philistines had captured the ark of God, they took it from Ebenezer to Ashdod. Then they carried the ark into Dagon's temple and set it beside Dagon. When the people of Ashdod rose early the next day, there was Dagon, fallen on his face on the ground before the ark of the Lord! They took Dagon and put him back in his place. But the following morning when they rose, there was Dagon, fallen on his face on the ground before the ark of the Lord! His head and hands had been broken off and were lying on the threshold; only his body remained".

1 Samuel 7: 3-4 "So Samuel said to all the Israelites, "If you are returning to the Lord with all your hearts, then rid yourselves of the foreign gods and the Ashtoreths and commit yourselves to the Lord and serve him only, and he will deliver you out of the hand of the Philistines." So, the Israelites put away their Baals and Ashtoreths, and served the Lord only".

1 Samuel 8: 8 "As they have done from the day, I brought them up out of Egypt until this day, forsaking me and serving other gods, so they are doing to you".

1 Samuel 12: 10, 21-22 "They cried out to the Lord and said, 'We have sinned; we have forsaken the Lord and served the Baals and the Ashtoreths. But now deliver us from the hands of our enemies, and we will serve you" ... Do not turn away after useless idols. They can do you no good, nor can they rescue you, because they are useless. For the sake of his great name the LORD will not reject his people, because the LORD was pleased to make you his own".

XVI. The Book of I Kings

1 Kings 8: 60 "so that all the peoples of the earth may know that the LORD is God and that there is no other".

1 kings 9: 6-9 "But if you or your descendants turn away from me and do not observe the commands and decrees I have given you and go off to serve other gods and worship them, then I will cut off Israel from the land I have given them and will reject this temple I have consecrated for my Name... People will answer, 'Because they have forsaken the LORD their God, who brought their ancestors out of Egypt, and have embraced other gods, worshiping and serving them—that is why the LORD brought all this disaster on them".

1 Kings 11: 4-10, 33 "As Solomon grew old, his wives turned his heart after other gods, and his heart was not fully devoted to the LORD his God, as the heart of David his father had been. He followed Ashtoreth the goddess of the Sidonians, and Molek the detestable god of the Ammonites. So, Solomon did evil in the eyes of the LORD; he did not follow the LORD completely, as David his father had done. On a hill east of Jerusalem, Solomon built a high place for Chemosh the detestable god of Moab, and for Molek the detestable god of the Ammonites. He did the same for all his foreign wives, who burned incense and offered sacrifices to their gods. The LORD became angry with Solomon because his heart had turned away from the LORD, the God of Israel, who had appeared to him twice. Although he had forbidden Solomon to follow other gods, Solomon did not keep the LORD's command" ... I will do this because they have forsaken me and worshiped Ashtoreth the goddess of the Sidonians, Chemosh the god of the Moabites, and Molek the god of the Ammonites, and have not walked in obedience to me, nor done what is right in my eyes, nor kept my decrees and laws as David, Solomon's father, did".

1 Kings 12: 26-33 "Jeroboam thought to himself, "The kingdom will now likely revert to the house of David. If these people go up to offer sacrifices at the temple of the LORD in Jerusalem, they will again give their allegiance to their lord, Rehoboam king of Judah. They will kill me and return to King Rehoboam." After seeking advice, the king made two golden calves. He said to the people, "It is too much for you to go up to Jerusalem. Here are your gods, Israel, who brought you up out of Egypt." One he set up in Bethel, and the other in Dan. And this thing became a sin; the people came to worship the one at Bethel and went as far as Dan to worship the other. Jeroboam built shrines on high places and appointed priests from all sorts of people, even though they were not Levites. He instituted a festival on the fifteenth day of the eighth month, like the festival held in Judah, and offered sacrifices on the altar. This he did in Bethel, sacrificing to the calves he had made. And at Bethel he also installed priests at the high places he had made. On the fifteenth day of the eighth month, a month of his own choosing, he offered sacrifices on the altar he had built at Bethel. So, he instituted the festival for the Israelites and went up to the altar to make offerings".

1 Kings 13: 4-5, 32-34 "When King Jeroboam heard what the man of God cried out against the altar at Bethel, he stretched out his hand from the altar and said, "Seize him!" But the hand he stretched out toward the man shriveled up, so that he could not pull it back. Also, the altar was split apart, and its ashes poured out according to the sign given by the man of God by the word of the LORD… For the message he declared by the word of the LORD against the altar in Bethel and against all the shrines on the high places in the towns of Samaria will certainly come true." Even after this, Jeroboam did not change his evil ways, but once more appointed priests for the high places from all sorts of people. Anyone who wanted to become a priest he consecrated for the high places. This was the sin of the house of Jeroboam that led to its downfall and to its destruction from the face of the earth".

1 kings 14: 9-12, 23-24 "You have done more evil than all who lived before you. You have made for yourself other gods, idols made of metal; you have aroused my anger and turned your back on me. "Because of this, I am going to bring disaster on the house of Jeroboam…They also set up for themselves high places, sacred stones and Asherah poles on every high hill and under every spreading tree. There were even male shrine prostitutes in the land; the people engaged in all the detestable practices of the nations the LORD had driven out before the Israelites".

1 kings 15: 11-14 "Asa did what was right in the eyes of the LORD, as his father David had done. He expelled the male shrine prostitutes from the land and got rid of all the idols his ancestors had made. He even deposed his grandmother Maakah from her position as queen mother, because she had made a repulsive image for the worship of Asherah. Asa cut it down and burned it in the Kidron Valley. Although he did not remove the high places, Asa's heart was fully committed to the LORD all his life".

1 kings 16: 13, 25-26, 31-33 "because of all the sins Baasha and his son Elah had committed and had caused Israel to commit, so that they aroused the anger of the LORD, the God of Israel, by their worthless idols… But Omri did evil in the eyes of the LORD and sinned more than all those before him. He followed completely the ways of Jeroboam son of Nebat, committing the same sin Jeroboam had caused Israel to commit, so that they aroused the anger of the LORD, the God of Israel, by their worthless idols" … He not only considered it trivial to commit the sins of Jeroboam son of Nebat, but he also married Jezebel daughter of Ethbaal king of the Sidonians and began to serve Baal and worship him. He set up an altar for Baal in the temple of Baal that he built in Samaria. Ahab also made an Asherah pole and did more to arouse the anger of the Lord, the God of Israel, than did all the kings of Israel before him".

1 Kings 18: 18-19, 22-38 "I have not made trouble for Israel," Elijah replied. "But you and your father's family have. You have abandoned the Lord's commands and have followed the Baals. Now summon the people from all over Israel to meet me on Mount Carmel. And bring the four hundred and fifty prophets of Baal and the four hundred prophets of Asherah, who eat at Jezebel's table" ... Then Elijah said to them, "I am the only one of the Lord's prophets left, but Baal has four hundred and fifty prophets. Get two bulls for us. Let Baal's prophets choose one for themselves and let them cut it into pieces and put it on the wood but not set fire to it. I will prepare the other bull and put it on the wood but not set fire to it. Then you call on the name of your god, and I will call on the name of the Lord. The god who answers by fire—he is God." Then all the people said, "What you say is good." Elijah said to the prophets of Baal, "Choose one of the bulls and prepare it first, since there are so many of you. Call on the name of your god, but do not light the fire." So, they took the bull given them and prepared it. Then they called on the name of Baal from morning till noon. "Baal, answer us!" they shouted. But there was no response; no one answered. And they danced around the altar they had made. At noon Elijah began to taunt them. "Shout louder!" he said. "Surely he is a god! Perhaps he is deep in thought, or busy, or traveling. Maybe he is sleeping and must be awakened." So, they shouted louder and slashed themselves with swords and spears, as was their custom, until their blood flowed. Midday passed, and they continued their frantic prophesying until the time for the evening sacrifice. But there was no response, no one answered, no one paid attention. Then Elijah said to all the people, "Come here to me." They came to him, and he repaired the altar of the Lord, which had been torn down. Elijah took twelve stones, one for each of the tribes descended from Jacob, to whom the word of the Lord had come, saying, "Your name shall be Israel." With the stones he built an altar in the name of the Lord, and he dug a trench around it large enough to hold two seahs of seed. He arranged the wood, cut the bull into pieces and laid it on the wood. Then he said to them, "Fill four large jars with water and pour it on the offering and on the wood." "Do it again," he said, and they did it again. "Do it a third time," he ordered, and they did it the third time. The water ran down around the altar and even filled the trench. At the time of sacrifice, the prophet Elijah stepped forward and prayed: "Lord, the God of Abraham, Isaac and Israel, let it be known today that you are God in Israel and that I am your servant and have done all these things at your command. Answer me, Lord, answer me, so these people will know that you, Lord, are God, and that you are turning their hearts back again." Then the fire of the Lord fell and burned up the sacrifice, the wood, the stones and the soil, and also licked up the water in the trench".

1 Kings 19: 18 "Yet I reserve seven thousand in Israel—all whose knees have not bowed down to Baal and whose mouths have not kissed him."

1 Kings 21: 25-26 "(There was never anyone like Ahab, who sold himself to do evil in the eyes of the LORD, urged on by Jezebel his wife. He behaved in the vilest manner by going after idols, like the Amorites the LORD drove out before Israel.)"

1 Kings 21: 43, 53 "In everything he followed the ways of his father Asa and did not stray from them; he did what was right in the eyes of the LORD. The high places, however, were not removed, and the people continued to offer sacrifices and burn incense there." King Ahaziah… "served and worshiped Baal and aroused the anger of the LORD, the God of Israel, just as his father had done".

XVII. The book of 2 Kings

2 Kings 5 : 17-18 "If you will not," said Naaman, "please let me, your servant, be given as much earth as a pair of mules can carry, for your servant will never again make burnt offerings and sacrifices to any other god but the LORD. But may the LORD forgive your servant for this one thing: When my master enters the temple of Rimmon to bow down and he is leaning on my arm and I have to bow there also—when I bow down in the temple of Rimmon, may the LORD forgive your servant for this."

2 Kings 6: 20-29 "Jehu said, "Call an assembly in honor of Baal." So, they proclaimed it. Then he sent word throughout

Israel, and all the servants of Baal came; not one stayed away. They crowded into the temple of Baal until it was full from one end to the other. And Jehu said to the keeper of the wardrobe, "Bring robes for all the servants of Baal." So, he brought out robes for them. Then Jehu and Jehonadab son of Rekab went into the temple of Baal. Jehu said to the servants of Baal, "Look around and see that no one who serves the Lord is here with you—only servants of Baal." So, they went in to make sacrifices and burnt offerings. Now Jehu had posted eighty men outside with this warning: "If one of you lets any of the men, I am placing in your hands escape, it will be your life for his life." As soon as Jehu had finished making the burnt offering, he ordered the guards and officers: "Go in and kill them; let no one escape." So they cut them down with the sword. The guards and officers threw the bodies out and then entered the inner shrine of the temple of Baal. They brought the sacred stone out of the temple of Baal and burned it. They demolished the sacred stone of Baal and tore down the temple of Baal, and people have used it for a latrine to this day. So, Jehu destroyed Baal worship in Israel. However, he did not turn away from the sins of Jeroboam son of Nebat, which he had caused Israel to commit—the worship of the golden calves at Bethel and Dan".

2 Kings 12: 2-3 "Joash did what was right in the eyes of the Lord all the years Jehoiada the priest instructed him. The high places, however, were not removed; the people continued to offer sacrifices and burn incense there".

2 Kings 13: 6 "But they did not turn away from the sins of the house of Jeroboam, which he had caused Israel to commit; they continued in them. Also, the Asherah pole remained standing in Samaria".

2 Kings 15: 3-4, 34-35 "He did what was right in the eyes of the LORD, just as his father Amaziah had done. The high places, however, were not removed; the people continued to offer sacrifices and burn incense there" ... He did what was right in the eyes of the LORD, just as his father Uzziah had done. The high places, however, were not removed; the people continued to offer sacrifices and burn incense there. Jotham rebuilt the Upper Gate of the temple of the LORD".

2 Kings 16: 3-4 "He followed the ways of the kings of Israel and even sacrificed his son in the fire, engaging in the detestable practices of the nations the LORD had driven out before the Israelites. He offered sacrifices and burned incense at the high places, on the hilltops and under every spreading tree".

2 Kings 16 :10-14 "Then King Ahaz went to Damascus to meet Tiglath-Pileser king of Assyria. He saw an altar in Damascus and sent to Uriah the priest a sketch of the altar, with detailed plans for its construction. So, Uriah the priest built an altar in accordance with all the plans that King Ahaz had sent from Damascus and finished it before King Ahaz returned. When the king came back from Damascus and saw the altar, he approached it and presented offerings on it. He offered up his burnt offering and grain offering, poured out his drink offering, and splashed the blood of his fellowship offerings against the altar. As for the bronze altar that stood before the LORD, he brought it from the front of the temple—from between the new altar and the temple of the LORD—and put it on the north side of the new altar".

2 Kings 17:9-12, 15-17, 29-41 "The Israelites secretly did things against the LORD their God that were not right. From watchtower to fortified city they built themselves high places in all their towns. They set up sacred stones and Asherah poles on every high hill and under every spreading tree. At every high place they burned incense, as the nations whom the LORD had driven out before them had done. They did wicked things that aroused the LORD's anger. They worshiped idols, though the LORD had said, "You shall not do this...They rejected his decrees and the covenant he had made with their ancestors and the statutes he had warned them to keep. They followed worthless idols and themselves became worthless. They imitated the nations around them although the LORD had ordered them, "Do not do as they do." They forsook all the commands of the LORD their God and made for themselves two idols cast in the shape of calves, and an Asherah pole. They bowed down to all the starry hosts, and they worshiped Baal. They sacrificed their sons and daughters in the fire. They practiced divination and sought omens and sold themselves to do evil in the eyes of the LORD, arousing his anger... Nevertheless, each national group made its own gods in the several towns where they settled and set them up in the shrines the people of Samaria had made at the high places. The people from Babylon made Sukkoth Benoth, those from Kuthah made Nergal, and those from Hamath made Ashima; the Avvites made Nibhaz and Tartak, and the Sepharvites burned their children in the fire as sacrifices to Adrammelek and Anammelek, the gods of Sepharvaim. They worshiped the LORD, but they also appointed all sorts of their own people to officiate for them as priests in the shrines at the high places. They worshiped the LORD, but they also served their own gods in accordance with the customs of the nations from which they had been brought. To this day they persist in their former practices. They neither worship the LORD nor adhere to the decrees and regulations, the laws and commands that the LORD gave the descendants of Jacob, whom he named Israel. When the LORD made a covenant with the Israelites, he commanded them: "Do not worship any other gods or bow down to them, serve them or sacrifice to them. But the LORD, who brought you up out of Egypt with mighty power and outstretched arm, is the one you must worship. To him you shall bow down and to him offer sacrifices. You must always be careful to keep the decrees and regulations, the laws and commands he wrote for you. Do not worship other gods. Do not forget the covenant I have made with you, and do not worship other gods. Rather, worship the LORD your God; it is he who will deliver you from the hand of all your enemies. They would not listen, however, but persisted in their former practices. Even while these people were worshiping the LORD, they were serving their idols. To this day their children and grandchildren continue to do as their ancestors did".

2 Kings 18: 3-4 "He did what was right in the eyes of the LORD, just as his father David had done. He removed the high places, smashed the sacred stones and cut down the Asherah poles. He broke into pieces the bronze snake Moses had made, for up to that time the Israelites had been burning incense to it. (It was called Nehushtan".

2 Kings 19: 18 "They have thrown their gods into the fire and destroyed them, for they were not gods but only wood and stone, fashioned by human hands".

2 Kings 21:2-11, 20-21 "He did evil in the eyes of the LORD, following the detestable practices of the nations the LORD had driven out before the Israelites. He rebuilt the high places his father Hezekiah had destroyed; he also erected altars to Baal and made an Asherah pole, as Ahab king of Israel had done. He bowed down to all the starry hosts and worshiped them. He built altars in the temple of the LORD, of which the LORD had said, "In Jerusalem I will put my Name." In the two courts of the temple of the LORD, he built altars to all the starry hosts. He sacrificed his own son in the fire, practiced divination, sought omens, and consulted mediums and spiritists. He did much evil in the eyes of the LORD, arousing his anger. He took the carved Asherah pole he had made and put it in the temple, of which the LORD had said to David and to his son Solomon, "In this temple and in Jerusalem, which I have chosen out of all the tribes of Israel, I will put my Name forever. I will not again make the feet of the Israelites wander from the land I gave their ancestors, if only they will be careful to do everything, I commanded them and will keep the whole Law that my servant Moses gave them." But the people did not listen. Manasseh led them astray, so that they did more evil than the nations the LORD had destroyed before the Israelites. The LORD said through his servants the prophets: "Manasseh king of Judah has committed these detestable sins. He has done more evil than the Amorites who preceded him and has led Judah into sin with his idols… He did evil in the eyes of the LORD, as his father Manasseh had done. He followed completely the ways of his father, worshiping the idols his father had worshiped, and bowing down to them".

2 Kings 22: 17 "Because they have forsaken me and burned incense to other gods and aroused my anger by all the idols their hands have made, my anger will burn against this place and will not be quenched".

2 Kings 23: 4-7 "The king ordered Hilkiah the high priest, the priests next in rank and the doorkeepers to remove from the temple of the LORD all the articles made for Baal and Asherah and all the starry hosts. He burned them outside Jerusalem in the fields of the Kidron Valley and took the ashes to Bethel. He did away with the idolatrous priests appointed by the kings of Judah to burn incense on the high places of the towns of Judah and on those around Jerusalem—those who burned incense to Baal, to the sun and moon, to the constellations and to all the starry hosts. He took the Asherah pole from the temple of the LORD to the Kidron Valley outside Jerusalem and burned it there. He ground it to powder and scattered the dust over the graves of the common people. He also tore down the quarters of the male shrine prostitutes that were in the temple of the LORD, the quarters where women did weaving for Asherah".

XVIII.   1 Chronicles & 2 Chronicles

1 Chronicles 16: 25-26

> "For great is the LORD and most
>   worthy of praise; he is to be feared above all
>   gods.
> For all the gods of the nations are idols"

2 Chronicles 2: 5-6 "The temple I am going to build will be great, because our God is greater than all other gods. But who is able to build a temple for him, since the heavens, even the highest heavens, cannot contain him? Who then am I to build a temple for him, except as a place to burn sacrifices before him?"

2 Chronicles 7: 19-22 "But if you turn away and forsake the decrees and commands I have given you and go off to serve other gods and worship them, then I will uproot Israel from my land, which I have given them, and will reject this temple I have consecrated for my Name. I will make it a byword and an object of ridicule among all peoples. This temple will become a heap of rubble. All who pass by will be appalled and say, 'Why has the LORD done such a thing to this land and to this temple?' People will answer, 'Because they have forsaken the LORD, the God of their ancestors, who brought them out of Egypt, and have embraced other gods, worshiping and serving them—that is why he brought all this disaster on them".

2 Chronicles 13:8-9 "And now you plan to resist the kingdom of the LORD, which is in the hands of David's descendants. You are indeed a vast army and have with you the golden calves that Jeroboam made to be your gods. But didn't you drive out the priests of the LORD, the sons of Aaron, and the Levites, and make priests of your own as the peoples of other lands do? Whoever comes to consecrate himself with a young bull and seven rams may become a priest of what are not gods".

2 Chronicles 15: 16 -17 "King Asa also deposed his grandmother Maakah from her position as queen mother, because she had made a repulsive image for the worship of Asherah. Asa cut it down, broke it up and burned it in the Kidron Valley. Although he did not remove the high places from Israel, Asa's heart was fully committed to the LORD all his life".

2 Chronicles 23: 16-17 "Jehoiada then made a covenant that he, the people and the king would be the LORD's people. All the people went to the temple of Baal and tore it down. They smashed the altars and idols and killed Mattan the priest of Baal in front of the altars".

2 Chronicles 25: 14-15 "When Amaziah returned from slaughtering the Edomites, he brought back the gods of the people of Seir. He set them up as his own gods, bowed down to them and burned sacrifices to them. The anger of the LORD burned against Amaziah, and he sent a prophet to him, who said, "Why do you consult this people's gods, which could not save their own people from your hand?"

2 Chronicles 28: 2-4, 22-25 "He followed the ways of the kings of Israel and also made idols for worshiping the Baals. He burned sacrifices in the Valley of Ben Hinnom and sacrificed his children in the fire, engaging in the detestable practices of the nations the LORD had driven out before the Israelites. He offered sacrifices and burned incense at the high places, on the hilltops and under every spreading tree... In his time of trouble King Ahaz became even more unfaithful to the LORD. He offered sacrifices to the gods of Damascus, who had defeated him; for he thought, "Since the gods of the kings of Aram have helped them, I will sacrifice to them so they will help me." But they were his downfall and the downfall of all Israel. Ahaz gathered together the furnishings from the temple of God and cut them in pieces. He shut the doors of the LORD's temple and set up altars at every street corner in Jerusalem. In every town in Judah he built high places to burn sacrifices to other gods and aroused the anger of the LORD, the God of his ancestors".

2 Chronicles 33: 3-17 "He rebuilt the high places his father Hezekiah had demolished; he also erected altars to the Baals and made Asherah poles. He bowed down to all the starry hosts and worshiped them. He built altars in the temple of the LORD, of which the LORD had said, "My Name will remain in Jerusalem forever." In both courts of the temple of the LORD, he built altars to all the starry hosts. He sacrificed his children in the fire in the Valley of Ben Hinnom, practiced divination and witchcraft, sought omens, and consulted mediums and spiritists. He did much evil in the eyes of the LORD, arousing his anger. He took the image he had made and put it in God's temple, of which God had said to David and to his son Solomon, "In this temple and in Jerusalem, which I have chosen out of all the tribes of Israel, I will put my Name forever. I will not again make the feet of the Israelites leave the land I assigned to your ancestors, if only they will be careful to do everything, I commanded them concerning all the laws, decrees and regulations given through Moses." But Manasseh led Judah and the people of Jerusalem astray, so that they did more evil than the nations the LORD had destroyed before the Israelites. The LORD spoke to Manasseh and his people, but they paid no attention. So, the LORD brought against them the army commanders of the king of Assyria, who took Manasseh prisoner, put a hook in his nose, bound him with bronze shackles and took him to Babylon. In his distress he sought the favor of the LORD his God and humbled himself greatly before the God of his ancestors. And when he prayed to him, the LORD was moved by his entreaty and listened to his plea; so, he brought him back to Jerusalem and to his kingdom. Then Manasseh knew that the LORD is God. Afterward he rebuilt the outer wall of the City of David, west of the Gihon spring in the valley, as far as the entrance of the Fish Gate and encircling the hill of Ophel; he also made it much higher. He stationed military commanders in all the fortified cities in Judah. He got rid of the foreign gods and removed the image from the temple of the Lord, as well as all the altars he had built on the temple hill and in Jerusalem; and he threw them out of the city. Then he restored the altar of the Lord and sacrificed fellowship offerings and thank offerings on it, and told Judah to serve the Lord, the God of Israel. The people, however, continued to sacrifice at the high places, but only to the Lord their God".

2 Chronicles 34: 25, 33 "Because they have forsaken me and burned incense to other gods and aroused my anger by all that their hands have made, my anger will be poured out on this place and will not be quenched…' Josiah removed all the detestable idols from all the territory belonging to the Israelites, and he had all who were present in Israel serve the Lord their God. As long as he lived, they did not fail to follow the Lord, the God of their ancestors".

XIX. The Book of Job & Psalms

Job 31: 26-28 "if I have regarded the sun in its radiance or the moon moving in splendor, so that my heart was secretly enticed and my hand offered them a kiss of homage, then these also would be sins to be judged, for I would have been unfaithful to God on high".

Psalms 4:2-3

> "How long will you people turn my glory into shame?
>> How long will you love delusions and seek false gods?
>
> Know that the LORD has set apart his faithful servant for himself;
>> the LORD hears when I call to him".

Psalm 78: 58

> "They angered him with their high places;
>> they aroused his jealousy with their idols".

Psalm 81: 8-9

> "Hear me, my people, and I will warn you—
>> if you would only listen to me, Israel!
>
> You shall have no foreign god among you;
>> you shall not worship any god other than me".

Psalm 95: 3

> "For the LORD is the great God,
>> the great King above all gods"

Psalm 96: 4-5

> "For great is the LORD and most worthy of praise;
>> he is to be feared above all gods.
>
> For all the gods of the nations are idols,
>> but the LORD made the heavens".

Psalm 97: 9

"For you, Lord, are the Most High over all the earth;

you are exalted far above all gods".

Psalm 106: 19, 28, 34-37

"At Horeb they made a calf
and worshiped an idol cast from metal.

They exchanged their glorious God
for an image of a bull, which eats grass...
They yoked themselves to the Baal of Peor

and ate sacrifices offered to lifeless gods;
but they mingled with the nations and adopted their customs.

They worshiped their idols, which became a snare to them.

They sacrificed their sons and their daughters to false gods".

Psalm 115: 2-8

"Why do the nations say, "Where is their God?

Our God is in heaven; he does whatever pleases him.

But their idols are silver and gold, made by human hands.

They have mouths, but cannot speak, eyes, but cannot see.

They have ears, but cannot hear, noses, but cannot smell.

They have hands, but cannot feel, feet, but cannot walk,
nor can they utter a sound with their throats.
Those who make them will be like them,
and so, will all who trust in them".

Psalm 135: 15-18

"The idols of the nations are silver and gold, made by human hands.
They have mouths, but cannot speak, eyes, but cannot see.
They have ears, but cannot hear, nor is there breath in their mouths.
Those who make them will be like them,
and so will all who trust in them".

XX. The book of Isaiah

Isaiah 2: 8, 17-18, 20-21

"Their land is full of idols; they bow down to the work of their hands,
to what their fingers have made...
The arrogance of man will be brought low and human pride humbled;
the LORD alone will be exalted in that day,
and the idols will totally disappear...

> In that day people will throw away to the moles and bats
>
> their idols of silver and idols of gold, which they made to worship.
>
> > They will flee to caverns in the rocks and to the overhanging crags
> >
> > > from the fearful presence of the Lord and the splendor of his majesty,
>
> when he rises to shake the earth".

Isaiah 30:22

> "Then you will desecrate your idols overlaid with silver
>
> > and your images covered with gold;
>
> you will throw them away like a menstrual cloth
>
> > and say to them, "Away with you!"

Isaiah 31: 7

> "Return, you Israelites, to the One you have so greatly revolted against.
>
> > For in that day every one of you will reject the idols of silver
>
> and gold your sinful hands have made".

Isaiah 40: 18-20

> "With whom, then, will you compare God?
> > To what image will you liken him?
> As for an idol, a metalworker casts it,
> > and a goldsmith overlays it with gold

and fashions silver chains for it.

> A person too poor to present such an offering selects wood that will not rot;
>> they look for a skilled worker to set up an idol that will not topple".

Isaiah 41: 21-24, 28-29

> "Present your case," says the LORD.
>> "Set forth your arguments," says Jacob's King.
>
> "Tell us, you idols, what is going to happen.
> Tell us what the former things were,
>> so that we may consider them and know their final outcome.
>
> Or declare to us the things to come,
>> tell us what the future holds, so we may know that you are gods.
>
> Do something, whether good or bad,
>> so that we will be dismayed and filled with fear.
>
> But you are less than nothing and your works are utterly worthless;
>> whoever chooses you is detestable…
>
> I look but there is no one— no one among the gods to give counsel,
>> no one to give answer when I ask them.
>
> See, they are all false!
>> Their deeds amount to nothing;
>
> their images are but wind and confusion".

Isaiah 42: 8, 17

> "I am the Lord; that is my name!
> I will not yield my glory to another or my praise to idols...
> But those who trust in idols, who say to images,
> 'You are our gods,' will be turned back in utter shame".

Isaiah 43: 9-13

> "All the nations gather together and the peoples assemble.
> Which of their gods foretold this and proclaimed to us the former things?
> Let them bring in their witnesses to prove they were right,
> so that others may hear and say, "It is true."
> "You are my witnesses," declares the Lord,
> "and my servant whom I have chosen,
> so that you may know and believe me and understand that I am he.
> Before me no god was formed, nor will there be one after me.
> I, even I, am the Lord, and apart from me there is no savior.
> I have revealed and saved and proclaimed—
> I, and not some foreign god among you.
> You are my witnesses," declares the Lord, "that I am God.
> Yes, and from ancient days I am he.

No one can deliver out of my hand.
When I act, who can reverse it?"

Isaiah 44: 9-20 (see Chapter I)

Isaiah 45: 16, 20

"All the makers of idols will be put to shame and disgraced;
    they will go off into disgrace together. ...
Ignorant are those who carry about idols of wood,
    who pray to gods that cannot save".

Isaiah 46: 1-2, 6-7

"Bel bows down, Nebo stoops low;
    their idols are borne by beasts of burden.
The images that are carried about are burdensome,
    a burden for the weary.
They stoop and bow down together; unable to rescue the burden,
    they themselves go off into captivity...
Some pour out gold from their bags
    and weigh out silver on the scales;
they hire a goldsmith to make it into a god,
    and they bow down and worship it.
They lift it to their shoulders and carry it;
    they set it up in its place, and there it stands.
From that spot it cannot move.

> Even though someone cries out to it, it cannot answer;
>
> it cannot save them from their troubles".

Isaiah 48: 5, 13-14

> "Therefore, I told you these things long ago; before they happened,
>
> > I announced them to you so that you could not say,
>
> 'My images brought them about;
> > my wooden image and metal god ordained them.'...
>
> My own hand laid the foundations of the earth,
> > and my right hand spread out the heavens;
>
> when I summon them, they all stand up together.
>
> > "Come together, all of you, and listen:
>
> Which of the idols has foretold these things?
> > The LORD's chosen ally will carry out his purpose against Babylon;
>
> his arm will be against the Babylonians".

Isaiah 57: 8, 13 (See chapter 3)

Isaiah 65: 7

> "both your sins and the sins of your ancestors," says the LORD.
>
> > "Because they burned sacrifices on the mountains and defied me on the hills,

I will measure into their laps the full payment for
their former deeds."

Isaiah 66: 3

"...and whoever burns memorial incense
is like one who worships an idol.
They have chosen their own ways,
and they delight in their abominations"

XXI. The Book of Jeremiah

Jeremiah 1: 16

"I will pronounce my judgments on my people
because of their wickedness in forsaking me,
in burning incense to other gods
and in worshiping what their hands have made".

Jeremiah 2: 5, 8, 11, 25

"This is what the LORD says:
"What fault did your ancestors find in me,
that they strayed so far from me?
They followed worthless idols and became worthless
themselves. ...
Those who deal with the law did not know me;
the leaders rebelled against me.
The prophets prophesied by Baal, following
worthless idols…

Has a nation ever changed its gods? (Yet they are not gods at all.)
> But my people have exchanged their glorious God for worthless idols…

Do not run until your feet are bare and your throat is dry.
But you said, 'It's no use! I love foreign gods, and I must go after them.'"…

Jeremiah 2: 27- 28 (See chapter 3)

Jeremiah 3: 6-9, 13

"During the reign of King Josiah, the LORD said to me, "Have you seen what faithless Israel has done? She has gone up on every high hill and under every spreading tree and has committed adultery there. I thought that after she had done all this she would return to me but she did not, and her unfaithful sister Judah saw it. I gave faithless Israel her certificate of divorce and sent her away because of all her adulteries. Yet I saw that her unfaithful sister Judah had no fear; she also went out and committed adultery. Because Israel's immorality mattered so little to her, she defiled the land and committed adultery with stone and wood" … Only acknowledge your guilt— you have rebelled against the LORD your God, you have scattered your favors to foreign gods under every spreading tree, and have not obeyed me,'" declares the LORD".

Jeremiah 4: 1
> "If you, Israel, will return, then return to me," declares the LORD.
>> "If you put your detestable idols out of my sight and no longer go astray..."

Jeremiah 7: 9-10, 18-19, 30-31 "Will you steal and murder, commit adultery and perjury, burn incense to Baal and follow other gods you have not known, and then come and stand before me in this house, which bears my Name, and say, "We are safe"—safe to do all these detestable things? Has this house, which bears my Name, become a den of robbers to you? But I have been watching! declares the LORD... The children gather wood, the fathers light the fire, and the women knead the dough and make cakes to offer to the Queen of Heaven. They pour out drink offerings to other gods to arouse my anger. But am I the one they are provoking? declares the LORD. Are they not rather harming themselves, to their own shame?... "The people of Judah have done evil in my eyes, declares the LORD. They have set up their detestable idols in the house that bears my Name and have defiled it. They have built the high places of Topheth in the Valley of Ben Hinnom to burn their sons and daughters in the fire—something I did not command, nor did it enter my mind".

Jeremiah 8: 19
> "Why have they aroused my anger with their images, with their worthless foreign idols?"

Jeremiah 9: 13-14 "The Lord said, "It is because they have forsaken my law, which I set before them; they have not obeyed me or followed my law. Instead, they have followed the stubbornness of their hearts; they have followed the Baals, as their ancestors taught them."

Jeremiah 10: 3-5, 8-9, 11, 14-15
"For the practices of the peoples are worthless;
   they cut a tree out of the forest, and a craftsman shapes it with his chisel.
They adorn it with silver and gold;
   they fasten it with hammer and nails so it will not totter.
Like a scarecrow in a cucumber field, their idols cannot speak;
   they must be carried because they cannot walk.
   Do not fear them;
they can do no harm, nor can they do any good." …
   They are all senseless and foolish;
they are taught by worthless wooden idols.
   Hammered silver is brought from Tarshish and gold from Uphaz.
What the craftsman and goldsmith have made is then dressed in blue and purple—
   all made by skilled workers…
"Tell them this: 'These gods, who did not make the heavens and the earth,
   will perish from the earth and from under the heavens'" …

> Everyone is senseless and without knowledge;
>> every goldsmith is shamed by his idols.
> The images he makes are a fraud; they have no breath in them.
>
> They are worthless, the objects of mockery;
>> when their judgment comes, they will perish"

Jeremiah 11: 10-13, 17 "They have returned to the sins of their ancestors, who refused to listen to my words. They have followed other gods to serve them. Both Israel and Judah have broken the covenant I made with their ancestors. Therefore, this is what the LORD says: 'I will bring on them a disaster they cannot escape. Although they cry out to me, I will not listen to them. The towns of Judah and the people of Jerusalem will go and cry out to the gods to whom they burn incense, but they will not help them at all when disaster strikes. You, Judah, have as many gods as you have towns; and the altars you have set up to burn incense to that shameful god Baal are as many as the streets of Jerusalem.'... The LORD Almighty, who planted you, has decreed disaster for you, because the people of both Israel and Judah have done evil and aroused my anger by burning incense to Baal".

Jeremiah 13: 10 "These wicked people, who refuse to listen to my words, who follow the stubbornness of their hearts and go after other gods to serve and worship them, will be like this belt—completely useless!"

Jeremiah 13: 25
"This is your lot, the portion I have decreed for you," declares the LORD, "because you have forgotten me and trusted in false gods.
I will pull up your skirts over your face that your shame may be seen"

Jeremiah 14: 14 "Then the LORD said to me, "The prophets are prophesying lies in my name. I have not sent them or appointed them or spoken to them. They are prophesying to you false visions, divinations, idolatries and the delusions of their own minds".

Jeremiah 14: 22
"Do any of the worthless idols of the nations bring rain?
Do the skies themselves send down showers?
No, it is you, LORD our God. Therefore, our hope is in you, for you are the one who does all this".

Jeremiah 16: 11, 13, 18 "then say to them, 'It is because your ancestors forsook me,' declares the LORD, 'and followed other gods and served and worshiped them. They forsook me and did not keep my law.... So I will throw you out of this land into a land neither you nor your ancestors have known, and there you will serve other gods day and night, for I will show you no favor...' I will repay them double for their wickedness and their sin, because they have defiled my land with the lifeless forms of their vile images and have filled my inheritance with their detestable idols."

Jeremiah 16: 19-20

"LORD, my strength and my fortress,
>my refuge in time of distress,
to you the nations will come from the ends of the earth and say,
>"Our ancestors possessed nothing but false gods,
worthless idols that did them no good.
>Do people make their own gods? Yes, but they are not gods!"

Jeremiah 18: 15 "Yet my people have forgotten me; they burn incense to worthless idols, which made them stumble in their ways, in the ancient paths. They made them walk in byways, on roads not built up".

Jeremiah 19: 4-5, 13 "For they have forsaken me and made this a place of foreign gods; they have burned incense in it to gods that neither they nor their ancestors nor the kings of Judah ever knew, and they have filled this place with the blood of the innocent. They have built the high places of Baal to burn their children in the fire as offerings to Baal—something I did not command or mention, nor did it enter my mind... The houses in Jerusalem and those of the kings of Judah will be defiled like this place, Topheth—all the houses where they burned incense on the roofs to all the starry hosts and poured out drink offerings to other gods".

Jeremiah 22:8-9 "…Why has the LORD done such a thing to this great city?' And the answer will be: 'Because they have forsaken the covenant of the LORD their God and have worshiped and served other gods'".

Jeremiah 32: 29-30, 34-35 "The Babylonians who are attacking this city will come in and set it on fire; they will burn it down, along with the houses where the people aroused my anger by burning incense on the roofs to Baal and by pouring out drink offerings to other gods. "The people of Israel and Judah have done nothing but evil in my sight from their youth; indeed, the people of Israel have done nothing but arouse my anger with what their hands have made, declares the LORD" … They set up their vile images in the house that bears my Name and defiled it. They built high places for Baal in the Valley of Ben Hinnom to sacrifice their sons and daughters to Molek, though I never commanded—nor did it enter my mind—that they should do such a detestable thing and so make Judah sin".

Jeremiah 35: 15 "Again and again I sent all my servants the prophets to you. They said, "Each of you must turn from your wicked ways and reform your actions; do not follow other gods to serve them. Then you will live in the land I have given to you and your ancestors." But you have not paid attention or listened to me".

Jeremiah 44: 4-5, 8, 15-28 "gain and again I sent my servants the prophets, who said, 'Do not do this detestable thing that I hate!' But they did not listen or pay attention; they did not turn from their wickedness or stop burning incense to other gods... Why arouse my anger with what your hands have made, burning incense to other gods in Egypt, where you have come to live? You will destroy yourselves and make yourselves a curse and an object of reproach among all the nations on earth... Then all the men who knew that their wives were burning incense to other gods, along with all the women who were present—a large assembly—and all the people living in Lower and Upper Egypt, said to Jeremiah, "We will not listen to the message you have spoken to us in the name of the LORD! We will certainly do everything we said we would: We will burn incense to the Queen of Heaven and will pour out drink offerings to her just as we and our ancestors, our kings and our officials did in the towns of Judah and in the streets of Jerusalem. At that time, we had plenty of food and were well off and suffered no harm. But ever since we stopped burning incense to the Queen of Heaven and pouring out drink offerings to her, we have had nothing and have been perishing by sword and famine." The women added, "When we burned incense to the Queen of Heaven and poured out drink offerings to her, did not our husbands know that we were making cakes impressed with her image and pouring out drink offerings to her?" Then Jeremiah said to all the people, both men and women, who were answering him, "Did not the LORD remember and call to mind the incense burned in the towns of Judah and the streets of Jerusalem by you and your ancestors, your kings and your officials and the people of the land? When the LORD could no longer endure your wicked actions and the detestable things you did, your land became a curse and a desolate waste without inhabitants, as it is today. Because you have burned incense and have sinned against the Lord and have not obeyed him or followed his law or his decrees or his stipulations, this disaster has come upon you, as you now see." Then Jeremiah said to all the people, including the women, "Hear the word of the Lord, all you people of Judah in Egypt. This is what the Lord Almighty, the God of Israel, says: You and your wives have done what you said you would do when you promised, 'We will certainly carry out the vows we made to burn incense and pour out drink offerings to the Queen of Heaven.' "Go ahead then, do what you promised! Keep your vows! But hear the word of the Lord, all you Jews living in Egypt: 'I swear by my great name,' says the Lord, 'that no one from Judah living anywhere in Egypt will ever again invoke my name or swear, "As surely as the Sovereign Lord lives." For I am watching over them for harm, not for good; the Jews in Egypt will perish by sword and famine until they are all destroyed. Those who escape the sword and return to the land of Judah from Egypt will be very few. Then the whole remnant of Judah who came to live in Egypt will know whose word will stand—mine or theirs".

Jeremiah 50: 2-3, 38

"Announce and proclaim among the nations,
lift up a banner and proclaim it; keep nothing
back, but say,
'Babylon will be captured; Bel will be put to shame,
Marduk filled with terror.

> Her images will be put to shame and her idols
> filled with terror.'

A nation from the north will attack her and lay waste her land.

> No one will live in it; both people and animals
> will flee away...

A drought on her waters! They will dry up.
For it is a land of idols, idols that will go mad with terror".

Jeremiah 51: 17-18, 47, 52

"Everyone is senseless and without knowledge;
every goldsmith is shamed by his idols.

> The images he makes are a fraud;
> they have no breath in them.

They are worthless, the objects of mockery;
> when their judgment comes, they will perish" ...
> For the time will surely come when
> I will punish the idols of Babylon;

her whole land will be disgraced,
and her slain will all lie fallen within her...

> "But days are coming," declares the LORD,
> "when I will punish her idols,

and throughout her land the wounded will groan".

XXII. The Book of Ezekiel

Ezekiel 5: 8-11 "Therefore this is what the Sovereign Lord says: I myself am against you, Jerusalem, and I will inflict punishment on you in the sight of the nations. Because of all your detestable idols, I will do to you what I have never done before and will never do again. Therefore, in your midst parents will eat their children, and children will eat their parents. I will inflict punishment on you and will scatter all your survivors to the winds. Therefore as surely as I live, declares the Sovereign Lord, because you have defiled my sanctuary with all your vile images and detestable practices, I myself will shave you; I will not look on you with pity or spare you".

Ezekiel 6: 5-7, 9 "I will lay the dead bodies of the Israelites in front of their idols, and I will scatter your bones around your altars. Wherever you live, the towns will be laid waste and the high places demolished, so that your altars will be laid waste and devastated, your idols smashed and ruined, your incense altars broken down, and what you have made wiped out… Then in the nations where they have been carried captive, those who escape will remember me—how I have been grieved by their adulterous hearts, which have turned away from me, and by their eyes, which have lusted after their idols. They will loathe themselves for the evil they have done and for all their detestable practices".

Ezekiel 7: 20
> "They took pride in their beautiful jewelry
> and used it to make their detestable idols.
> They made it into vile images;
> therefore, I will make it a thing unclean for them".

Ezekiel 11: 18, 21 "They will return to it and remove all its vile images and detestable idols" ... But as for those whose hearts are devoted to their vile images and detestable idols, I will bring down on their own heads what they have done, declares the Sovereign Lord."

Ezekiel 14: 3-8 "Son of man, these men have set up idols in their hearts and put wicked stumbling blocks before their faces. Should I let them inquire of me at all? Therefore speak to them and tell them, 'This is what the Sovereign Lord says: When any of the Israelites set up idols in their hearts and put a wicked stumbling block before their faces and then go to a prophet, I the Lord will answer them myself in keeping with their great idolatry. I will do this to recapture the hearts of the people of Israel, who have all deserted me for their idols.' "Therefore, say to the people of Israel, 'This is what the Sovereign Lord says: Repent! Turn from your idols and renounce all your detestable practices!' "When any of the Israelites or any foreigner residing in Israel separate themselves from me and set up idols in their hearts and put a wicked stumbling block before their faces and then go to a prophet to inquire of me, I the Lord will answer them myself. I will set my face against them and make them an example and a byword. I will remove them from my people. Then you will know that I am the LORD".

Ezekiel: 16: 17-31, 35-36 "You also took the fine jewelry I gave you, the jewelry made of my gold and silver, and you made for yourself male idols and engaged in prostitution with them. And you took your embroidered clothes to put on them, and you offered my oil and incense before them. Also, the food I provided for you—the flour, olive oil and honey I gave you to eat—you offered as fragrant incense before them. That is what happened, declares the Sovereign LORD. "'And you took your sons and daughters whom you bore to me and sacrificed them as food to the idols. Was your prostitution not enough? You slaughtered my children and sacrificed them to the idols. In all your detestable practices and your prostitution, you did not remember the days of your youth, when you were naked and bare, kicking about in your blood." 'Woe! Woe to you, declares the Sovereign LORD. In addition to all your other wickedness, you built a mound for yourself and made a lofty shrine in every public square. At every street corner you built your lofty shrines and degraded your beauty, spreading your legs with increasing promiscuity to anyone who passed by. You engaged in prostitution with the Egyptians, your neighbors with large genitals, and aroused my anger with your increasing promiscuity. So, I stretched out my hand against you and reduced your territory; I gave you over to the greed of your enemies, the daughters of the Philistines, who were shocked by your lewd conduct. You engaged in prostitution with the Assyrians too, because you were insatiable; and even after that, you still were

not satisfied. Then you increased your promiscuity to include Babylonia, a land of merchants, but even with this you were not satisfied. "'I am filled with fury against you, declares the Sovereign LORD, when you do all these things, acting like a brazen prostitute! When you built your mounds at every street corner and made your lofty shrines in every public square, you were unlike a prostitute, because you scorned payment...
"'Therefore, you prostitute, hear the word of the LORD! This is what the Sovereign LORD says: Because you poured out your lust and exposed your naked body in your promiscuity with your lovers, and because of all your detestable idols, and because you gave them your children's blood" ...

Ezekiel 18: 5-6, 9, 10-13, 15

> "Suppose there is a righteous man who does what is just and right.
>> He does not eat at the mountain shrines or look to the idols of Israel....
> He follows my decrees and faithfully keeps my laws.
>> That man is righteous; he will surely live, declares the Sovereign LORD...
> "Suppose he has a violent son, who sheds blood

or does any of these other things (though the father has done none of them):

> "He eats at the mountain shrines. He defiles his neighbor's wife.

He oppresses the poor and needy. He commits robbery.
> He does not return what he took in pledge. He looks to the idols…
> Will such a man live? He will not!

Because he has done all these detestable things,
> he is to be put to death; his blood will be on his own head".

"But suppose this son has a son who sees all the sins his father commits,
> and though he sees them, he does not do such things:
> "He does not eat at the mountain shrines or look to the idols of Israel.

He does not defile his neighbor's wife.
> He does not oppress anyone or require a pledge for a loan.

He does not commit robbery but gives his food to the hungry
> and provides clothing for the naked.
> He withholds his hand from mistreating the poor and takes no interest or profit from them.
> He keeps my laws and follows my decrees.

He will not die for his father's sin; he will surely live".

Ezekiel 20: 7-8, 16, 18, 24, 28, 32, 39 "And I said to them, "Each of you, get rid of the vile images you have set your eyes on, and do not defile yourselves with the idols of Egypt. I am the LORD your God." "'But they rebelled against me and would not listen to me; they did not get rid of the vile images they had set their eyes on, nor did they forsake the idols of Egypt. So I said I would pour out my wrath on them and spend my anger against them in Egypt... because they rejected my laws and did not follow my decrees and desecrated my Sabbaths. For their hearts were devoted to their idols.... I said to their children in the wilderness, "Do not follow the statutes of your parents or keep their laws or defile yourselves with their idols... because they had not obeyed my laws but had rejected my decrees and desecrated my Sabbaths, and their eyes lusted after their parents' idols... When I brought them into the land, I had sworn to give them and they saw any high hill or any leafy tree, there they offered their sacrifices, made offerings that aroused my anger, presented their fragrant incense and poured out their drink offerings... "'You say, "We want to be like the nations, like the peoples of the world, who serve wood and stone." But what you have in mind will never happen... "'As for you, people of Israel, this is what the Sovereign LORD says: Go and serve your idols, every one of you! But afterward you will surely listen to me and no longer profane my holy name with your gifts and idols".

Ezekiel 22: 2-4, 8-9 "Son of man, will you judge her? Will you judge this city of bloodshed? Then confront her with all her detestable practices and say: 'This is what the Sovereign LORD says: You city that brings on herself doom by shedding blood in her midst and defiles herself by making idols, you have become guilty because of the blood you have shed and have become defiled by the idols you have made. You have brought your days to a close, and the end of your years has come. Therefore, I will make you an object of scorn to the nations and a laughingstock to all the countries... You have despised my holy things and desecrated my Sabbaths. In you are slanderers who are bent on shedding blood; in you are those who eat at the mountain shrines and commit lewd acts".

Ezekiel 23: 7, 30, 36-39 "She gave herself as a prostitute to all the elite of the Assyrians and defiled herself with all the idols of everyone she lusted after... have brought this on you, because you lusted after the nations and defiled yourself with their idols... The LORD said to me: "Son of man, will you judge Oholah and Oholibah? Then confront them with their detestable practices, for they have committed adultery and blood is on their hands. They committed adultery with their idols; they even sacrificed their children, whom they bore to me, as food for them. They have also done this to me: At that same time they defiled my sanctuary and desecrated my Sabbaths. On the very day they sacrificed their children to their idols, they entered my sanctuary and desecrated it. That is what they did in my house".

Ezekiel 30: 13

"This is what the Sovereign LORD says:
"I will destroy the idols and put an end to the images in Memphis.
No longer will there be a prince in Egypt,
and I will spread fear throughout the land".

Ezekiel 33: 25 "Therefore say to them, 'This is what the Sovereign LORD says: Since you eat meat with the blood still in it and look to your idols and shed blood, should you then possess the land?"

Ezekiel 36: 18, 25 "So I poured out my wrath on them because they had shed blood in the land and because they had defiled it with their idols… I will sprinkle clean water on you, and you will be clean; I will cleanse you from all your impurities and from all your idols".

Ezekiel 37: 23 "hey will no longer defile themselves with their idols and vile images or with any of their offenses, for I will save them from all their sinful backsliding, and I will cleanse them. They will be my people, and I will be their God".

Ezekiel 44: 10-14 "'The Levites who went far from me when Israel went astray and who wandered from me after their idols must bear the consequences of their sin. They may serve in my sanctuary, having charge of the gates of the temple and serving in it; they may slaughter the burnt offerings and sacrifices for the people and stand before the people and serve them. But because they served them in the presence of their idols and made the people of Israel fall into sin, therefore I have sworn with uplifted hand that they must bear the consequences of their sin, declares the Sovereign LORD. They are not to come near to serve me as priests or come near any of my holy things or my most holy offerings; they must bear the shame of their detestable practices. And I will appoint them to guard the temple for all the work that is to be done in it".

XXIII. The Book of Daniel

Daniel 3: 3-18, 28-29 "So the satraps, prefects, governors, advisers, treasurers, judges, magistrates and all the other provincial officials assembled for the dedication of the image that King Nebuchadnezzar had set up, and they stood before it. Then the herald loudly proclaimed, "Nations and peoples of every language, this is what you are commanded to do: As soon as you hear the sound of the horn, flute, zither, lyre, harp, pipe and all kinds of music, you must fall down and worship the image of gold that King Nebuchadnezzar has set up. Whoever does not fall down and worship will immediately be thrown into a blazing furnace." Therefore, as soon as they heard the sound of the horn, flute, zither, lyre, harp and all kinds of music, all the nations and peoples of every language fell down and worshiped the image of gold that King Nebuchadnezzar had set up. At this time some astrologers came forward and denounced the Jews. They said to King Nebuchadnezzar, "May the king live forever! Your Majesty has issued a decree that everyone who hears the sound of the horn, flute, zither, lyre, harp, pipe and all kinds of music must fall down and worship the image of gold, and that whoever does not fall down and worship will be thrown into a blazing furnace. But there are some Jews whom you have set over the affairs of the province of Babylon—Shadrach, Meshach and Abednego—who pay no attention to you, Your Majesty. They neither serve your gods nor worship the image of gold you have set up." Furious with rage, Nebuchadnezzar summoned Shadrach, Meshach and Abednego. So these men were brought before the king, and Nebuchadnezzar said to them, "Is it true, Shadrach, Meshach and Abednego, that you do not serve my gods or worship the image of gold I have set up? Now when you hear the sound of the horn, flute, zither, lyre, harp, pipe and all kinds of music, if you are ready to fall down and worship the image I made, very good. But if you do not worship it, you will be thrown immediately into a blazing furnace. Then what god will be able to rescue you from my hand?" Shadrach, Meshach and Abednego replied to him, "King Nebuchadnezzar, we do not need to defend ourselves before you in this matter. If we are thrown into the blazing furnace, the God we serve is able to deliver us from it, and he will deliver us from Your Majesty's hand. But even if he does not, we want you to know, Your Majesty, that we will not serve your gods or worship the image of gold you have set up." ... Then Nebuchadnezzar said, "Praise be to the God of Shadrach, Meshach and Abednego, who has sent his angel and rescued his servants! They trusted in him and defied the king's command and were willing to give up their lives rather than serve or worship any god except their own God. Therefore, I decree that the people of any nation or language who say anything against the God of Shadrach, Meshach and Abednego be cut into pieces and their houses be turned into piles of rubble, for no other god can save in this way."

Ezekiel 5: 4, 23 "As they drank the wine, they praised the gods of gold and silver, of bronze, iron, wood and stone… Instead, you have set yourself up against the Lord of heaven. You had the goblets from his temple brought to you, and you and your nobles, your wives and your concubines drank wine from them. You praised the gods of silver and gold, of bronze, iron, wood and stone, which cannot see or hear or understand. But you did not honor the God who holds in his hand your life and all your ways. Therefore, he sent the hand that wrote the inscription".

XXIV. The Book of Hosea

Hosea 2: 8, 13, 17

"She has not acknowledged that I was the one who gave her the grain,
   the new wine and oil, who lavished on her
the silver and gold— which they used for Baal…
   I will punish her for the days she burned incense to the Baals;
she decked herself with rings and jewelry,
   and went after her lovers,
but me she forgot," declares the Lord…
   I will remove the names of the Baals from her lips;
no longer will their names be invoked".

Hosea 3:1, 4 "The Lord said to me, "Go, show your love to your wife again, though she is loved by another man and is an adulteress. Love her as the Lord loves the Israelites, though they turn to other gods and love the sacred raisin cakes." ... For the Israelites will live many days without king or prince, without sacrifice or sacred stones, without ephod or household gods".

Hosea 4: 7-9, 12-17

"The more priests there were, the more they sinned against me;
> they exchanged their glorious God for something disgraceful.

They feed on the sins of my people and relish their wickedness.
> And it will be: Like people, like priests.
> I will punish both of them for their ways and repay them for their deeds" ...

My people consult a wooden idol, and a diviner's rod speaks to them.
> A spirit of prostitution leads them astray; they are unfaithful to their God.

They sacrifice on the mountaintops and burn offerings on the hills,
> under oak, poplar and terebinth, where the shade is pleasant.
> Therefore, your daughters turn to prostitution

and your daughters-in-law to adultery.

> "I will not punish your daughters when they turn to prostitution,
>
> nor your daughters-in-law when they commit adultery,
>
> > because the men themselves consort with harlots and sacrifice with shrine prostitutes—
>
> a people without understanding will come to ruin!
>
> > "Though you, Israel, commit adultery, do not let Judah become guilty.
>
> "Do not go to Gilgal; do not go up to Beth Aven.
>
> > And do not swear, 'As surely as the Lord lives!'
> >
> > The Israelites are stubborn, like a stubborn heifer.
>
> How then can the Lord pasture them like lambs in a meadow?
>
> > Ephraim is joined to idols; leave him alone!"

Hosea 7: 14: See chapter V

Hosea 8: 4, 6

> "They set up kings without my consent;
>
> > they choose princes without my approval.
>
> With their silver and gold, they make idols
>
> > for themselves to their own destruction.
>
> Samaria throw out your calf-idol! My anger burns against them.
>
> > How long will they be incapable of purity?...
> >
> > They are from Israel! This calf—a metalworker has made it;

it is not God. It will be broken in pieces, that calf of Samaria".

Hosea 9: 10

"When I found Israel, it was like finding grapes in the desert;
> when I saw your ancestors, it was like seeing the early fruit on the fig tree.

But when they came to Baal Peor, they consecrated themselves
> to that shameful idol and became as vile as the thing they loved".

Hosea 10: 5

"The people who live in Samaria fear for the calf-idol of Beth Aven.
> Its people will mourn over it, and so will its idolatrous priests,

those who had rejoiced over its splendor,
> because it is taken from them into exile".

Hosea 12: 11

"Is Gilead wicked? Its people are worthless!
> Do they sacrifice bulls in Gilgal?

Their altars will be like piles of stones on a plowed field"

Hosea 13: 1-2

"When Ephraim spoke, people trembled; he was exalted in Israel.

But he became guilty of Baal worship and died. Now they sin more and more;

they make idols for themselves from their silver, cleverly fashioned images, all of them the work of craftsmen.

It is said of these people, "They offer human sacrifices! They kiss calf-idols!"

Hosea 14: 3, 8

"Assyria cannot save us; we will not mount warhorses.

We will never again say 'Our gods' to what our own hands have made,

for in you the fatherless find compassion." …

Ephraim, what more have I to do with idols? I will answer him and care for him. I am like a flourishing juniper;

your fruitfulness comes from me."

XXV. The Book of Amos

Amos 2: 4

"This is what the Lord says:

"For three sins of Judah, even for four, I will not relent.
Because they have rejected the law of the LORD and have not kept his decrees,
> because they have been led astray by false gods,
> the gods their ancestors followed, …

They lie down beside every altar on garments taken in pledge.
> In the house of their god they drink wine taken as fines".

Amos 3: 14

"On the day I punish Israel for her sins,
> I will destroy the altars of Bethel;

the horns of the altar will be cut off and fall to the ground".

Amos 5: 26

"You have lifted up the shrine of your king,
> the pedestal of your idols, the star of your god—

which you made for yourselves".

Amos 8: 14

"Those who swear by the sin of Samaria— who say,
> 'As surely as your god lives, Dan,'

or, 'As surely as the god of Beersheba lives'—
> they will fall, never to rise again."

XXVI. The Book of Jonah, Micah, Nahum, Habakkuk, Zephaniah, Zechariah

Jonah 2: 8

"Those who cling to worthless idols
  turn away from God's love for them".

Micah 1: 7

"All her idols will be broken to pieces;
  all her temple gifts will be burned with fire; I will destroy all her images.
Since she gathered her gifts from the wages of prostitutes,
  as the wages of prostitutes, they will again be used".

Micah 5: 13-14

"I will destroy your idols and your sacred stones from among you;
  you will no longer bow down to the work of your hands.
I will uproot from among you your Asherah poles when I demolish your cities".

Micah 6: 16

"You have observed the statutes of Omri
  and all the practices of Ahab's house;
you have followed their traditions.

Therefore, I will give you over to ruin and your
people to derision;
you will bear the scorn of the nations".

Nahum 1: 14

"The LORD has given a command concerning you,
Nineveh:

"You will have no descendants to bear your name.
I will destroy the images and idols that are in the
temple of your gods.

I will prepare your grave, for you are vile."

Habakkuk 2: 18-19

"Of what value is an idol carved by a craftsman?
Or an image that teaches lies?
For the one who makes it trusts in his own creation;
he makes idols that cannot speak.
Woe to him who says to wood, 'Come to life!' Or to
lifeless stone,
'Wake up!' Can it give guidance?
It is covered with gold and silver; there is no breath
in it".

Zephaniah 1: 3-9

"I will sweep away both man and beast;
I will sweep away the birds in the sky and the fish
in the sea—
and the idols that cause the wicked to stumble."

"When I destroy all mankind on the face of the earth," declares the LORD,
> "I will stretch out my hand against Judah and against all who live in Jerusalem.
> I will destroy every remnant of Baal worship in this place,

the very names of the idolatrous priests—
> those who bow down on the roofs to worship the starry host,

those who bow down and swear by the LORD and who also swear by Molek,
> those who turn back from following the LORD
> and neither seek the LORD nor inquire of him."

Be silent before the Sovereign LORD, for the day of the LORD is near.
> The LORD has prepared a sacrifice; he has consecrated those he has invited.

"On the day of the LORD's sacrifice I will punish the officials
> and the king's sons and all those clad in foreign clothes.
> On that day I will punish all who avoid stepping on the threshold,

who fill the temple of their gods with violence and deceit?"

Zephaniah 2: 11

> "The LORD will be awesome to them
> > when he destroys all the gods of the earth.

> Distant nations will bow down to him,
>> all of them in their own lands".

Zechariah 10: 2

> "The idols speak deceitfully,
>> diviners see visions that lie;
>
> they tell dreams that are false,
>> they give comfort in vain.
>
> Therefore, the people wander like sheep
>> oppressed for lack of a shepherd".

Zechariah 13: 2 "On that day, I will banish the names of the idols from the land, and they will be remembered no more," declares the LORD Almighty. "I will remove both the prophets and the spirit of impurity from the land".

XXVII.   The Book of Acts, Romans, Corinthians

Acts 7: 40-49 "They told Aaron, 'Make us gods who will go before us. As for this fellow Moses who led us out of Egypt—we don't know what has happened to him!' That was the time they made an idol in the form of a calf. They brought sacrifices to it and reveled in what their own hands had made. But God turned away from them and gave them over to the worship of the sun, moon and stars. This agrees with what is written in the book of the prophets:

"'Did you bring me sacrifices and offerings
forty years in the wilderness, people of Israel?
You have taken up the tabernacle of Molek
and the star of your god Rephan,
the idols you made to worship.
Therefore I will send you into exile' beyond Babylon.

"Our ancestors had the tabernacle of the covenant law with them in the wilderness. It had been made as God directed Moses, according to the pattern he had seen. After receiving the tabernacle, our ancestors under Joshua brought it with them when they took the land from the nations God drove out before them. It remained in the land until the time of David, who enjoyed God's favor and asked that he might provide a dwelling place for the God of Jacob. But it was Solomon who built a house for him. "However, the Most High does not live in houses made by human hands. As the prophet says: "'Heaven is my throne, and the earth is my footstool. What kind of house will you build for me? says the Lord. Or where will my resting place be?".

Acts 14: 11-15 "When the crowd saw what Paul had done, they shouted in the Lycaonian language, "The gods have come down to us in human form!" Barnabas, they called Zeus, and Paul they called Hermes because he was the chief speaker. The priest of Zeus, whose temple was just outside the city, brought bulls and wreaths to the city gates because he and the crowd wanted to offer sacrifices to them. But when the apostles Barnabas and Paul heard of this, they tore their clothes and rushed out into the crowd, shouting: "Friends, why are you doing this? We too are only human, like you. We are bringing you good news, telling you to turn from these worthless things to the living God, who made the heavens and the earth and the sea and everything in them".

Acts 17: 16, 22-26 "While Paul was waiting for them in Athens, he was greatly distressed to see that the city was full of idols…Paul then stood up in the meeting of the Areopagus and said: "People of Athens! I see that in every way you are very religious. For as I walked around and looked carefully at your objects of worship, I even found an altar with this inscription: TO AN UNKNOWN GOD. So, you are ignorant of the very thing you worship—and this is what I am going to proclaim to you. "The God who made the world and everything in it is the Lord of heaven and earth and does not live in temples built by human hands. And he is not served by human hands, as if he needed anything. Rather, he himself gives everyone life and breath and everything else. From one man he made all the nations, that they should inhabit the whole earth; and he marked out their appointed times in history and the boundaries of their lands".

Acts 19: 23-27, 35- 38 "About that time there arose a great disturbance about the Way. A silversmith named Demetrius, who made silver shrines of Artemis, brought in a lot of business for the craftsmen there. He called them together, along with the workers in related trades, and said: "You know, my friends, that we receive a good income from this business. And you see and hear how this fellow Paul has convinced and led astray large numbers of people here in Ephesus and in practically the whole province of Asia. He says that gods made by human hands are no gods at all. There is danger not only that our trade will lose its good name, but also that the temple of the great goddess Artemis will be discredited; and the goddess herself, who is worshiped throughout the province of Asia and the world, will be robbed of her divine majesty."… The city clerk quieted the crowd and said: "Fellow Ephesians, doesn't all the world know that the city of Ephesus is the guardian of the temple of the great Artemis and of her image, which fell from heaven? Therefore, since these facts are undeniable, you ought to calm down and not do anything rash. You have brought these men here, though they have neither robbed temples nor blasphemed our goddess. If, then, Demetrius and his fellow craftsmen have a grievance against anybody, the courts are open and there are proconsuls. They can press charges".

Romans 1: 18-25 "The wrath of God is being revealed from heaven against all the godlessness and wickedness of people, who suppress the truth by their wickedness, since what may be known about God is plain to them, because God has made it plain to them. For since the creation of the world God's invisible qualities—his eternal power and divine nature—have been clearly seen, being understood from what has been made, so that people are without excuse. For although they knew God, they neither glorified him as God nor gave thanks to him, but their thinking became futile and their foolish hearts were darkened. Although they claimed to be wise, they became fools and exchanged the glory of the immortal God for images made to look like a mortal human being and birds and animals and reptiles. Therefore, God gave them over in the sinful desires of their hearts to sexual impurity for the degrading of their bodies with one another. They exchanged the truth about God for a lie and worshiped and served created things rather than the Creator—who is forever praised. Amen".

Romans 11: 4-13 "And what was God's answer to him? "I have reserved for myself seven thousand who have not bowed the knee to Baal."

1 Corinthians 8: 4- 13 "So then, about eating food sacrificed to idols: We know that "An idol is nothing at all in the world" and that "There is no God but one." For even if there are so-called gods, whether in heaven or on earth (as indeed there are many "gods" and many "lords"), yet for us there is but one God, the Father, from whom all things came and for whom we live; and there is but one Lord, Jesus Christ, through whom all things came and through whom we live. But not everyone possesses this knowledge. Some people are still so accustomed to idols that when they eat sacrificial food, they think of it as having been sacrificed to a god, and since their conscience is weak, it is defiled. But food does not bring us near to God; we are no worse if we do not eat, and no better if we do. Be careful, however, that the exercise of your rights does not become a stumbling block to the weak. For if someone with a weak conscience sees you, with all your knowledge, eating in an idol's temple, won't that person be emboldened to eat what is sacrificed to idols? So, this weak brother or sister, for whom

Christ died, is destroyed by your knowledge. When you sin against them in this way and wound their weak conscience, you sin against Christ. Therefore, if what I eat causes my brother or sister to fall into sin, I will never eat meat again, so that I will not cause them to fall".

1 Corinthians 10: 7, 14, 18-22 "Do not be idolaters, as some of them were; as it is written: "The people sat down to eat and drink and got up to indulge in revelry…Therefore, my dear friends, flee from idolatry… Consider the people of Israel: Do not those who eat the sacrifices participate in the altar? Do I mean then that food sacrificed to an idol is anything, or that an idol is anything? No, but the sacrifices of pagans are offered to demons, not to God, and I do not want you to be participants with demons. You cannot drink the cup of the Lord and the cup of demons too; you cannot have a part in both the Lord's table and the table of demons. Are we trying to arouse the Lord's jealousy? Are we stronger than he?".

1 Corinthians 12: 2 "You know that when you were pagans, somehow or other you were influenced and led astray to mute idols".

2 Corinthians 6: 16 "What agreement is there between the temple of God and idols? For we are the temple of the living God. As God has said: "I will live with them and walk among them, and I will be their God, and they will be my people".

XXVIII. The Book of Colossians, 1 Thessalonians, 1Peter, 1 John, Revelation

Colossians 2: 18-19 "Do not let anyone who delights in false humility and the worship of angels disqualify you. Such a person also goes into great detail about what they have seen; they are puffed up with idle notions by their unspiritual mind. They have lost connection with the head, from whom the whole body, supported and held together by its ligaments and sinews, grows as God causes it to grow".

1 Thessalonians 1: 7-10 "And so you became a model to all the believers in Macedonia and Achaia. The Lord's message rang out from you not only in Macedonia and Achaia—your faith in God has become known everywhere. Therefore, we do not need to say anything about it, for they themselves report what kind of reception you gave us. They tell how you turned to God from idols to serve the living and true God, and to wait for his Son from heaven, whom he raised from the dead—Jesus, who rescues us from the coming wrath".

1 Peter 4: 3 "For you have spent enough time in the past doing what pagans choose to do—living in debauchery, lust, drunkenness, orgies, carousing and detestable idolatry".

1 John 5: 8 "Dear children, keep yourselves from idols".

Revelation 9: 20 "The rest of mankind who were not killed by these plagues still did not repent of the work of their hands;

they did not stop worshiping demons, and idols of gold, silver, bronze, stone and wood—idols that cannot see or hear or walk".

Revelation 13: 11-15 "Then I saw a second beast, coming out of the earth. It had two horns like a lamb, but it spoke like a dragon. It exercised all the authority of the first beast on its behalf and made the earth and its inhabitants worship the first beast, whose fatal wound had been healed. And it performed great signs, even causing fire to come down from heaven to the earth in full view of the people. Because of the signs it was given power to perform on behalf of the first beast, it deceived the inhabitants of the earth. It ordered them to set up an image in honor of the beast who was wounded by the sword and yet lived. The second beast was given power to give breath to the image of the first beast, so that the image could speak and cause all who refused to worship the image to be killed".

Revelation 14: 9, 11 "A third angel followed them and said in a loud voice: "If anyone worships the beast and its image and receives its mark on their forehead or on their hand, they, too, will drink the wine of God's fury, which has been poured full strength into the cup of his wrath. They will be tormented with burning sulfur in the presence of the holy angels and of the Lamb. And the smoke of their torment will rise for ever and ever. There will be no rest day or night for those who worship the beast and its image, or for anyone who receives the mark of its name."

Revelation 15: 2-3 "those who had been victorious over the beast and its image and over the number of its name. They held harps given them by God and sang the song of God's servant Moses and of the Lamb"

Revelation 16: 2 "The first angel went and poured out his bowl on the land, and ugly, festering sores broke out on the people who had the mark of the beast and worshiped its image".

Revelation 19: 20 "But the beast was captured, and with it the false prophet who had performed the signs on its behalf. With these signs he had deluded those who had received the mark of the beast and worshiped its image. The two of them were thrown alive into the fiery lake of burning sulfur".

Revelation 20: 4-5 "I saw thrones on which were seated those who had been given authority to judge. And I saw the souls of those who had been beheaded because of their testimony about Jesus and because of the word of God. They had not worshiped the beast or its image and had not received its mark on their foreheads or their hands. They came to life and reigned with Christ a thousand years. (The rest of the dead did not come to life until the thousand years were ended.) This is the first resurrection. Blessed and holy are those who share in the first resurrection. The second death has no power over them, but they will be priests of God and of Christ and will reign with him for a thousand years".

Conclusion

GIVEN ALL THE EVIDENCE, IT is not too harsh to conclude that the Roman Catholic denomination was birthed by Satan to bring thorns and thistles into the work of salvation of Jesus Christ, our Lord, and Savior.

"Thou shall not carve an object and worship it" is a simple commandment of God. Nimrod defiled this command, and from generation to generation, his calls for humans to distance themselves from God and sabotage his work have been followed. To this very day, these practices are carried on in the most populous and duplicitous church of Jesus Christ—the Roman Catholic Church.

Other pagan religions worship Nimrod as well. Are their adepts blind to whom they worship like the Catholic votaries are? Regardless, they should put aside their hand-made gods, which have never spoken to them and never will. Those gods are nothing but useless objects of gold, wood, iron, or whatever materials are used. They remain mute, deaf, blind, and good for nothing but trash. The Apostle John stated in his first epistle, and I quote, "Dear children, keep yourselves from idols" (1 John 5:8).

In Jesus Christ, amen!

Acknowledgments

GOD IS GOOD AND ALL the time. Who am I, Lord, that you chose me as an instrument to further your kingdom? May your mighty name be glorified forever and ever. Amen!

I give thanks to Martino Publishing for giving me permission to cite Alexander Hislop's book entitled *The Two Babylons*. I extend my gratitude to my husband, Calvin, for his support; to our beloved daughter Ruth for her input in the cover design and drawing; and to the rest of our children: Anne Marie, Joash, Mercy, and Lydia.

References

Andrews, Evan. 2013. "Why Do We Kiss under the Mistletoe?" *History Stories* (blog), *History*. December 24, 2013. Last modified August 31, 2018. https://www.history.com/news/why-do-we-kiss-under-the-mistletoe .

Church of God International. 2020. "How Was Passover Replaced by Easter…and Who Did It?" https://www.cgi.org/new-page-56 .

Eveleth, Rose. 2012. "The History of Trick or Treating Is Weirder Than You Thought." *Smithsonian Magazine*. October 18, 2012. https://www.smithsonianmag.com/smart-news/the-history-of-trick-or-treating-is-weirder-than-you-thought-79408373/ .

Flynn, Tom. 1993. *The Trouble with Christmas Present and Yet to Come*. Buffalo, NY: Prometheus Books.

Hislop, Alexander. 2010. *The Two Babylons: Or the Papal Worship Proved to Be the Worship of Nimrod and His Wife*. Mansfield Centre, CT: Martino Publishing.

Jayaram. 2019. "Symbolism of Egg (Adam) in Hinduism." https://www.hinduwebsite.com/symbolism/symbols/egg.asp .

Mark, Joshua. 2009. Hathor https://www.ancient.eu/Hathor/

Merriam's Webster Dictionary. 2020. "Easter"

https://www.merriam-webster.com/dictionary/Easter

Rubio, J'aime. 2012. "Easter—Do You Really Know the Truth About It?" *Origins—"What Does History Say?"* (blog). July 5, 2012. https://whatdoeshistorysay.blogspot.com/2012/07/easter-do-you-really-know-truth-about.html .

Wikipedia. 2019. "Madonna (Art)." https://en.wikipedia.org/wiki/Madonna_(art)#Early_images .

Wikipedia. 2020. "Odin." https://en.wikipedia.org/wiki/Odin .

www.ingramcontent.com/pod-product-compliance
Lightning Source LLC
Chambersburg PA
CBHW071457040426
42444CB00008B/1375